I0020518

Stencyl Essentials

Build beautiful, unique, cross-platform games rapidly
with the free Stencyl 2D game engine and toolset

Richard Sneyd

BIRMINGHAM - MUMBAI

Stencyl Essentials

Copyright © 2015 Packt Publishing

First published: April 2015

Production reference: 1230415

Published by Packt Publishing Ltd.
Livery Place
35 Livery Street
Birmingham B3 2PB, UK.

ISBN 978-1-78439-945-0

www.packtpub.com

Cover image by Richard Sneyd (richardsneyd@hotmail.com)

Credits

Author
Richard Sneyd

Reviewers
Dan Bendell
Innes Borkwood
Jean-Marc "jihem" QUÉRÉ

Commissioning Editor
Kunal Parikh

Acquisition Editor
Richard Brookes-Bland

Content Development Editor
Ajinkya Paranjpe

Technical Editors
Rosmy George
Rohith Rajan

Copy Editor
Rashmi Sawant

Project Coordinator
Harshal Ved

Proofreaders
Martin Diver
Safis Editing
Paul Hindle

Indexer
Tejal Soni

Production Coordinator
Arvindkumar Gupta

Cover Work
Arvindkumar Gupta

About the Author

Richard Sneyd (BA Hons.) is the founder and CEO of CyberMyth Games, an indie game development studio based in Country Cork, Ireland. His role within the company requires that he wears many hats, including that of a programmer, designer, digital 2D and 3D artist, sound designer, scriptwriter, texture artist, leader, marketer, and business man.

He is also a fully registered, qualified, and highly experienced lecturer. His specialty subjects include 3D modeling and animation, computer game programming, 2D image processing, game design, desktop audio, psychology, consumer behavior, human resources, and business management. In addition to classroom teaching, he is actively involved in online education, regularly publishing new courses, and various other learning materials, such as books and tutorials, in conjunction with CyberMyth Games.

He is enthusiastic about his work, and his students and colleagues think of him as a very dedicated and accomplished teacher. All of his courses and books are characterized by a steady, incremental flow of information, and a lucid teaching style that is easy to understand and follow for all.

He is a husband to his wonderful wife, Jennifer, and father to a wonderful son, Darius.

Acknowledgements

I would like to take this opportunity to thank the Packt Publishing team for their outstanding work in helping to bring this book—my first ever published book—to fruition. I have thoroughly enjoyed working with them throughout the entire process and appreciate their candid encouragement and feedback, which ultimately raised the standard of my work. Along similar lines, I would like to thank the reviewers, Innes Borkwood, Daniel Bendell, and Jean-Marc "jihem" QUÉRÉ, whose poignant criticisms and observations have also served to raise the standard of the final product.

I also wish to acknowledge the tireless efforts of the Stencyl development team—principally, Jonathan Chung, founder of Stencyl Inc, as well as all of the hardworking members of the community who have contributed to the development of the Stencyl game engine and toolset. Thanks to their efforts, Stencyl has enabled a plethora of designers, artists, and hobbyists to realize their game ideas, which may not otherwise have been possible, and has evolved from its hopeful beginnings into the remarkable, cross-platform game development system that it is today.

I reserve my final acknowledgements for my beautiful wife, Jennifer, and my son, Darius, whose awesome baby cuddles made it all worthwhile. Without their patience, love, and support, none of this would have been possible. Thank you.

About the Reviewers

Dan Bendell is a budding young developer, currently studying computing and games development at the University of Plymouth. He is expected to complete his studies in 2016, after completing a year's work in the industry. On finishing his academic endeavors, he wishes to pursue his dream of either starting up a games development company or working at one, allowing him to create games that will truly engage his audience, as well as working with a variety of new people on a daily basis.

Jean-Marc "jihem" QUÉRÉ is a senior computer science engineer and is also the author of numerous articles in the French specialized press and books (on WinDev). Self-taught, he provided software for more than 20 years in every domain: decision-making methods, artificial learning, robotics, and autonomous systems. As a technology evangelist, he has chosen to support Livecode and Stencyl (since the migration from Flash to Haxe). He actively contributes to the community (extensions, translation, and support). Undoubtedly, you will meet him one day on the Stencyl forums. And you will be welcome!

www.PacktPub.com

Support files, eBooks, discount offers, and more

For support files and downloads related to your book, please visit www.PacktPub.com.

Did you know that Packt offers eBook versions of every book published, with PDF and ePub files available? You can upgrade to the eBook version at www.PacktPub.com and as a print book customer, you are entitled to a discount on the eBook copy. Get in touch with us at service@packtpub.com for more details.

At www.PacktPub.com, you can also read a collection of free technical articles, sign up for a range of free newsletters, and receive exclusive discounts and offers on Packt books and eBooks.

https://www2.packtpub.com/books/subscription/packtlib

Do you need instant solutions to your IT questions? PacktLib is Packt's online digital book library. Here, you can search, access, and read Packt's entire library of books.

Why subscribe?

- Fully searchable across every book published by Packt
- Copy and paste, print, and bookmark content
- On demand and accessible via a web browser

Free access for Packt account holders

If you have an account with Packt at www.PacktPub.com, you can use this to access PacktLib today and view 9 entirely free books. Simply use your login credentials for immediate access.

Table of Contents

Preface

The world of game development has been in a state of flux for the past few years. New technology, as well as new development tools and frameworks, has diversified the games industry and opened up the field to those who may not otherwise have been in a position to realize and publish their game concepts.

Stencyl is one such innovation. Developed from the ground up by founder Jonathan Chung, to be as accessible as possible to as many people as possible, yet it still retains the awesome power necessary for professional-level developers. Stencyl makes it possible for anyone with a great idea and the right motivation to develop their own games, from concept to market.

Stencyl Essentials has been written to get you up and running with Stencyl faster than with any other book, as it has been written in terse, yet lucid prose with a no-nonsense style, enabling you to get to grips with Stencyl in a fun, yet fast-paced way. This book is centered around a project, which has been designed to reinforce all of the key learning objectives. You will be guided through the process of building a game prototype, which is based on a successful, published game called Mudslide Cowboy (CyberMyth Games). By the end of this book, you will be competent in the use of all of Stencyl's most important features, and quite prepared to start working on your own game projects.

What this book covers

Chapter 1, *Exploring the Stencyl Toolset and Game Engine*, introduces the Stencyl toolset and interface, demonstrating how to navigate through all the most important screens.

Chapter 2, *Starting the Game Project*, explains the game concept, which we will be working on in the subsequent chapters, and guides you through the process of creating your first game project.

Chapter 3, Backgrounds and Tilesets, explains how to import Backgrounds and Tilesets and how to configure their settings, in preparation for use in our game levels.

Chapter 4, Building Levels Using Scenes, explains how you can learn to utilize backgrounds, foregrounds, and tiles to sculpt a visually compelling and varied game level.

Chapter 5, Actor Types and Instances, introduces you to the process of importing, customizing, and configuring actors, which can then be made interactive through using actor behaviors.

Chapter 6, Writing Simple Behaviors, teaches you the process of building the game logic using the signature block-snapping interface of the Behavior Designer in Stencyl.

Chapter 7, Complex Behaviors and Code, digs deep into the incredible power of Stencyl's visual programming system, showing you how to harness it at a more advanced level.

Chapter 8, Adding Sound Effects and Music, explains how Stencyl handles audio, and then guides you through the process of importing sound files, configuring them, and playing them in-game.

Chapter 9, Adding HUD Elements, shows how we can use actors in a special way to create animated elements of our heads-up display.

Chapter 10, Adding Menus and Buttons, guides you through the process of creating a Start screen and adding functional buttons to it.

Chapter 11, Scoring and Game Rules, helps you implement a game rule, based around the collection of gold coins, that will aid us in measuring success or failure during play sessions.

Chapter 12, Publishing and Monetization, gives us a clear overview of the principal publishing and monetization available to game developers in Stencyl.

What you need for this book

To get the most out of this book, you should at least have a basic understanding of computing. Ideally, you would also have some previous computer programming knowledge, although this is not completely essential. You will need to have access to a reasonably modern computer, with a reasonably modern operating system. For Windows users, Microsoft Windows XP or newer should do fine. I'd recommend at least 2 gigabytes of RAM, but preferably more. Mac OSX and Linux users should also be OK, as long they have a similar or superior amount of RAM.

Who this book is for

This book is mainly aimed at people who are familiar with computers, and have at least some basic computer programming experience. It has been designed to get you up and running with Stencyl in as little time as possible, so if you're looking for a no nonsense guide that will yield very fast results, this is the book for you.

Conventions

In this book, you will find a number of text styles that distinguish between different kinds of information. Here are some examples of these styles and an explanation of their meaning.

Code words in text, database table names, folder names, filenames, file extensions, pathnames, dummy URLs, user input, and Twitter handles are shown as follows: " When the download completes, you should have a file called `AlienApproach. stencyl`."

New terms and **important words** are shown in bold. Words that you see on the screen, for example, in menus or dialog boxes, appear in the text like this: "Clicking the **Next** button moves you to the next screen."

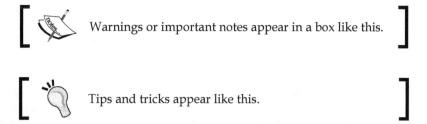

> Warnings or important notes appear in a box like this.

> Tips and tricks appear like this.

Reader feedback

Feedback from our readers is always welcome. Let us know what you think about this book — what you liked or disliked. Reader feedback is important for us as it helps us to develop titles that you will really get the most out of.

To send us general feedback, simply e-mail `feedback@packtpub.com`, and mention the book's title in the subject of your message.

If there is a topic that you have expertise in and you are interested in either writing or contributing to a book, see our author guide at `www.packtpub.com/authors`.

Customer support

Now that you are the proud owner of a Packt book, we have a number of things to help you to get the most from your purchase.

Downloading the example code

You can download the example code files from your account at http://www. packtpub.com for all the Packt Publishing books you have purchased. If you purchased this book elsewhere, you can visit http://www.packtpub.com/support and register to have the files e-mailed directly to you.

Downloading the color images of this book

We will also provide you with a PDF file that has color images of the screenshots/diagrams used in this book. The color images will help you better understand the changes in the output. You can download this file from: https://www.packtpub.com/sites/default/files/downloads/9450OT_ ColorImages.pdf.

Errata

Although we have taken every care to ensure the accuracy of our content, mistakes do happen. If you find a mistake in one of our books—maybe a mistake in the text or the code—we would be grateful if you could report this to us. By doing so, you can save other readers from frustration and help us improve subsequent versions of this book. If you find any errata, please report them by visiting http://www.packtpub. com/submit-errata, selecting your book, clicking on the **Errata Submission Form** link, and entering the details of your errata. Once your errata are verified, your submission will be accepted and the errata will be uploaded to our website or added to any list of existing errata under the Errata section of that title.

To view the previously submitted errata, go to https://www.packtpub.com/books/ content/support and enter the name of the book in the search field. The required information will appear under the **Errata** section.

Piracy

Piracy of copyrighted material on the Internet is an ongoing problem across all media. At Packt, we take the protection of our copyright and licenses very seriously. If you come across any illegal copies of our works in any form on the Internet, please provide us with the location address or website name immediately so that we can pursue a remedy.

Please contact us at copyright@packtpub.com, with a link to the suspected pirated material.

We appreciate your help in protecting our authors and our ability to bring you valuable content.

Questions

If you have a problem with any aspect of this book, you can contact us at questions@packtpub.com, and we will do our best to address the problem.

1
Exploring the Stencyl Toolset and Game Engine

Stencyl Essentials has been written as a no-nonsense, concise guide to acquiring the functional use of Stencyl in as little time as possible. To achieve this, little or no time is wasted discussing the basic computer science and/or programming concepts, as this fundamental knowledge is assumed on the part of the reader. In line with that, highly detailed instructions on how to download and install Stencyl will not be provided, as this is not considered to be a challenging process for someone with previous computer science experience. However, a simple, lucid outline of the process will be provided.

In this chapter, we will begin by downloading and installing the free version of Stencyl. The free version is all that is required to complete the lessons in this book. Immediately after that, we will begin exploring and rapidly become acquainted with the Stencyl interface, including all of the most important areas and layouts, which are as follows:

- Sign-in window
- The Welcome Center
- The Dashboard
- StencylForge
- Stencylpedia

By the end of this chapter, we will be comfortable enough to use Stencyl in order to be able to navigate through the most common screens, windows, and tabs at will and with relative ease. This newfound facility and comfort will stand us in good stead in the subsequent chapters, which will be fast-paced and punchy in the manner in which the new information is presented. Redundancy will be avoided wherever possible, which means there will not be a lot of needless posturing or repetition. So without further ado, let's start learning how to build games with Stencyl!

Downloading and installing Stencyl

Stencyl can very easily be downloaded free of charge from the official Stencyl website, www.stencyl.com. When you visit the landing page, you will see something that resembles the following screenshot:

Click on the **Download** button, which is prominently displayed on the landing page. You will then be given the option to download either a **Windows**, **Mac**, or **Linux** build:

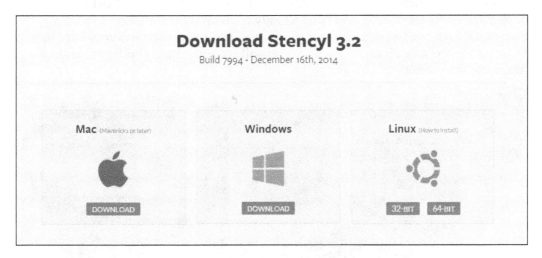

Simply select the appropriate build for your operating system, and click on **Download**. This could take anywhere from 20 seconds to 20 minutes depending on the speed of your Internet connection and the size of the particular Stencyl build you are downloading. Once the file is downloaded, launch the installer (if you are installing for Windows), follow all of the prompts, and when the installation is completed, you will have the option to launch Stencyl. If you have downloaded the Mac version, you will have to extract the `stencyl-full` folder from the downloaded ZIP file, then put it in the **Applications** directory for it to become useable. Once you have completed the appropriate steps, launch Stencyl.

For Linux users, the installation process may be a little more complicated. It is beyond the scope of this book to delve into such particulars. However, there is an excellent guide to the Ubuntu installation on the Stencyl website itself, which is available at `http://www.stencyl.com/help/view/install-stencyl-linux`.

Creating an account and signing in

When we first launch Stencyl, it will ask us to either sign in with an existing account or register a new account. If you have already registered for the Stencyl forums, then you do not need to create an account here. The same login credentials are used to access Stencyl as well as the forums. You will see something similar to this in the following screenshot:

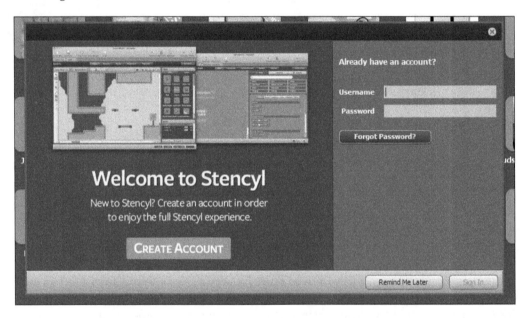

You need to complete one of these two tasks, obviously depending on whether you have a pre-existing account or not. Once this is done, we will be ready to explore the most important Stencyl screens and windows.

Exploring Stencyl – screens and windows

In this section, we will explore the most common fundamentals of the Stencyl screens and windows, briefly examining their basic nature and purpose, and learn how to navigate to them effectively and easily.

The Welcome Center

The **Welcome Center** is the first screen you will see after you first open Stencyl. Let's take a look at the following screenshot (your list of games will be different from mine; do not worry about this fact):

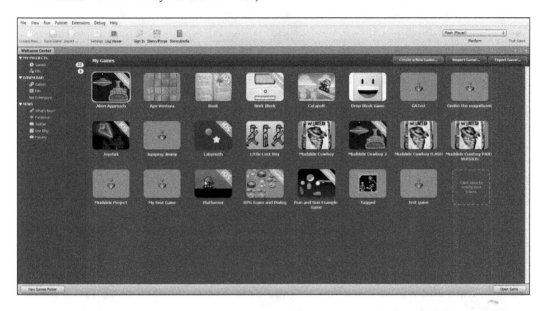

You may notice right off the bat that Stencyl does not have a native interface, whichever operating system you may be using (Windows, Mac, or Linux). In terms of style and aesthetics, it is entirely its own beast. The good news is that, because the toolset is written in Java, Stencyl looks much the same whether you're using it on Windows, Mac, or Linux. This is advantageous, as it is quite easy for us to jump from one OS to another without being disorientated by stylistic differences. What is more, games can be exported and imported between the installations of Stencyl as .stencyl files, across all the three supported operating systems, so you're never tied to just one OS. Let's look more closely at the important areas of this layout.

Drop-down menus

At the top-left corner of your **Welcome Center** layout, you will find a very familiar looking list of menus (see the following screenshot):

Here, we will find the very typical **File** menu that contains the menu items for common tasks, such as opening and closing games, importing resources (assets), importing and exporting games, signing in or out, and closing Stencyl. You will notice that some of the options in these menus are grayed out. This indicates that they cannot be clicked on in the current view. This is logical, as certain tasks can only be performed in appropriate contexts; for instance, it should be obvious that we can only click on **Close Game** when we already have one opened.

Next, we have our **View** menu, where we can switch between tabs, show or hide the **Toolbar** (the area that is shown at the bottom of the preceding screenshot), open up **StencylForge**, **Stencylpedia**, **Game Settings**, and the **Log Viewer**, all of which are important and will be discussed in good time. You will notice, as you scan the contents of the **View** menu, that the options have associated keyboard hotkeys. You may find it expedient to learn these, as it can improve your workflow with Stencyl in the long run.

The **Run** menu is only useful to us when we are inside a game project. It contains options for testing our game on various platforms, debugging tools, and so on. The **Publish**, **Extensions**, and **Debug** menus are likewise only really relevant when we have a game open. We cannot use them in the **Welcome Center**.

The toolbar

The toolbar, which is shown at the bottom of the previous screenshot, shows buttons for the following common tasks and windows:

- Create a new game
- Save a game
- Import
- Open the game settings window
- Show log viewer (primarily for debugging)
- Sign in
- Access StencylForge
- Open Stencylpedia

The Welcome Center tab

To the left of the layout, and as demonstrated by the following screenshot, we can see the **Welcome Center** tab (at the top-left corner of the window). All the screens in Stencyl are tabbed, so you can have several open at once. This includes scenes and actors, which we will learn about a little later on.

In the following screenshot, you will see that we have three drop-down menus:

- **My Projects**: Click on this tab to see your existing game projects, or any game kits (a starter pack for a certain type of a game) you have at your disposal.

- **Download**: When you click on **Sample Games**, it will take you to http://www.stencyl.com/developers/samples/. When you click on **Extensions**, it will take you to http://www.stencyl.com/developers/market/. Here, you can download extensions created by advanced Stencyl users, which add functionality to Stencyl.

- **News**: This is a collection of links that will take you to the social media pages related to Stencyl, the Stencyl **Blog**, or the **Forums**. The **Forums** are an excellent resource for one and all, as they enable all members of the community to share resources, ask and answer questions, collaborate on projects, and engage in idle, Stencyl, or game-related chit chat—all of which are good things. There is also a members-only area, where paying subscribers receive extra support and assistance from the Stencyl team.

Now, it is the right time to download a demo game so that we can use it to explore the Dashboard and other important areas of the Stencyl interface, which are only accessible from within a game:

1. Let's click on the **Sample Games** link.

2. When the Sample Games page opens in your browser, click on the download button for **Alien Approach**.

3. When the download completes, you should have a file called AlienApproach.stencyl. This file can be imported into Stencyl by navigating to **File | Import Game**. Then, you can navigate to the directory where you downloaded the sample game to (likely, your downloads folder).

4. Double-click on the file to import it. After a few moments, you should see a new game appear in your games list that looks similar to the following screenshot:

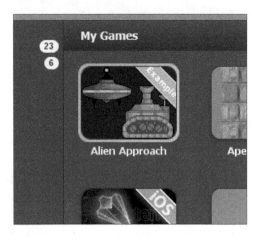

5. Double-click on the game to open it. We will use this sample game to explore our next major screen, the **Dashboard**.

A great way to get familiar with Stencyl quickly is to download all of the sample games we have seen earlier and tear them apart to see how they work.

The Dashboard

Once we have opened up our game, the **Welcome Center** disappears, and it is replaced with the **Dashboard**. This is the main view within our game. From here, we can access all of our game resources, such as **Scenes**, **Actor Types**, **Tilesets**, **Fonts**, **Behaviors**, and **Sounds**. In the following screenshot, you can see that these resource types are listed in the drop-down menu immediately below the **Dashboard** at the top-left corner of the page, under **Resources**:

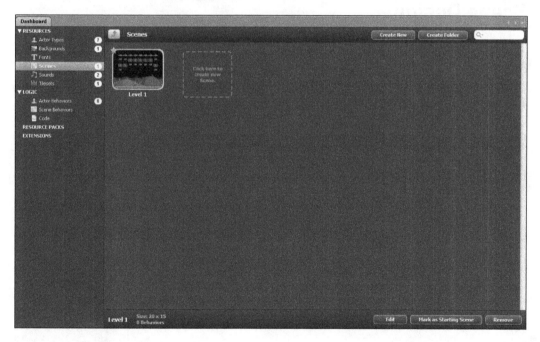

Let's very quickly click on each one of these resource types, starting with **Actor Types** and working down. You will see that as you do so, the contents of the main window changes; we are presented with a list of all assets of that particular type. When you've gotten as far as **Tilesets**, let's move on to the **Logic** drop-down menu immediately below it.

You will see that in this menu, we have three submenu items: **Actor Behaviors**, **Scene Behaviors**, and **Code**. **Actor Behaviors** are attached to **Actor Types** or individual instances of **Actors**, and modify their functionalities with conditional logic. They are akin to components, which you may have worked with in other game engines, such as **Unity**.

Scene Behaviors are similar, except that we attach them to **Scenes** instead of **Actors**. Clicking on **Code** will allow us to write our own classes. This is an advanced feature, which we rarely need to utilize, but it's good to be aware that the feature is available to us, as our abilities in Stencyl develop to a more advanced level.

Believe it or not, these nine menu items constitute all of the major asset types within our games. Once we have learned them all, and how they relate to and interact with each other, we will have a working knowledge of Stencyl and will be quite capable of building our own games!

Scene Designer

Let's go back to the scenes view by clicking on **Scenes** in our **Resources** menu. You will see that there is already one demo scene in this example game. Now, double-click on it to launch the scene designer and edit our scene. You will be presented with an additional tab with the name of your scene on it, beside the **Dashboard** tab, and a screen as shown in the following screenshot:

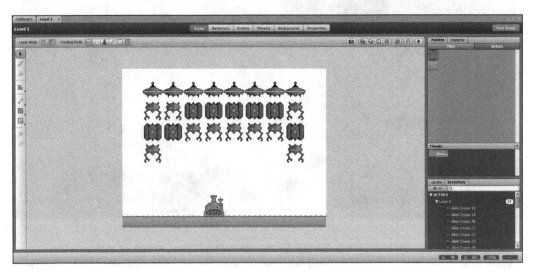

Let's take a closer look at the six tabs that we see at the top center of the screen:

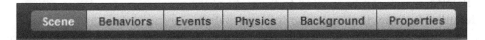

Clicking on any one of these will change our view to show tools and fields that relate directly to a certain aspect of our game. Here is a cursory breakdown of the different tabs and their relative significance in the crafting of a playable game level:

1. **Scene**: This is where we sculpt the level by placing tiles and actors on various layers. To the left of the screen, you will see a tool palette, which is similar in some respects to what you might find in a graphics manipulation tool, such as Photoshop or GIMP.

2. **Behaviors**: Here, we can add or remove **Scene Behaviors** as well as assign values to the exposed attributes; we'll be learning more about the attributes shortly. For now, just think of the term attribute as a synonym of the term variable, which is commonly used in math and programming vocabulary.

3. **Events**: While we usually use events within our behaviors, there are some instances where we may decide to create a single event that is associated directly with the scene object. In any case, we will not be using this tab as often as the **Behaviors** tab.

4. **Physics**: This is where we can set both horizontal and vertical gravity for our game level. How this gravity affects the individual actors within the scene will depend on how we have configured that specific actor's physics settings.

5. **Background**: This is where we can add backgrounds and foregrounds to our level, which can be repeated horizontally and vertically. If desired, we can also add parallax scrolling settings – an effect that is popular in platformer games.

6. **Properties**: This tab opens a window where we can alter certain basic scene properties, such as the **Name**, **Size**, and **Background color** (or gradient, if you should choose to use one).

Downloading the example code

You can download the example code files from your account at http://www.packtpub.com for all the Packt Publishing books you have purchased. If you purchased this book elsewhere, you can visit http://www.packtpub.com/support and register to have the files e-mailed directly to you.

The Palette

The **Palette**, which can be located to the right of the scene view (which is active by default when you first open the scene), is where we can go to select the tiles and/or actors we wish to paint onto the canvas. As you can see from the following screenshot, there are two tabs available to us within the palette — one shows the available actors, the other shows the available tiles that can be placed in our scene:

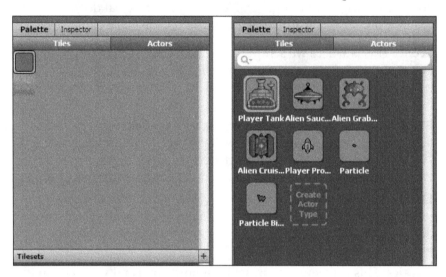

As we can see from the palette display, this particular game demo happens to contain only two tiles and seven actors in total. Some games can contain hundreds of each. If you take a look at the area above the palette area, you will see something similar to the following screenshot:

In the preceding screenshot, we have, from left to right and starting at the top, the following options:

- **Platform**: Flash is the default choice. Click on the button to see a drop-down menu displaying all your available options. Which options are displayed here will depend on what operating system you're using. If you're using Windows, for instance, the options will be **Flash (Player)**, **Flash (Browser)**, **Windows**, and **Android**.

- **Test Game**: By clicking on this tab, you can build and then attempt to launch the entire game for the specified target platform. The default scene, as identified by the star symbol, will be the first one to launch. Bring up the **Log Viewer** in tandem to view progress, warning, and error messages.

- **Test Scene**: Unlike the **Test Game** button, this only builds the current scene, and launches it directly, ignoring the rest of the game. The **Log Viewer** can be used for debugging purposes, as before.

The Log Viewer

Let's learn more about the **Log Viewer**. The easiest way to launch this tab is by clicking on the quick launch button, which has conveniently been placed on the toolbar for us; a permanent fixture at the top of the Stencyl interface. Let's click on that button now, and then click on the **Test Scene** button we learned about just moments ago. After a moment or so, you should see the following window appear (on Windows – the Mac version is a little different), and start to fill with lines of information:

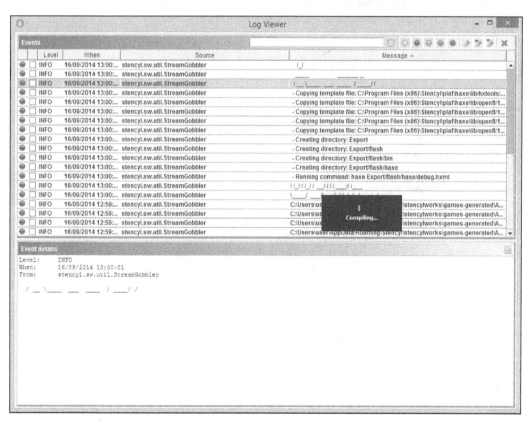

As you may have deduced, the information we are fed through the **Log Viewer** comes in the form of **Events**. These events, in turn, come in five basic categories:

1. **Debug**: These events are useful for debugging. We can trigger this type of event ourselves to assist in the debugging code.

2. **Info**: These events are helpful updates to let us know what is happening during the build or execution process of our program. They do not indicate a problem.

3. **Warning**: These events indicate a possible problem in the execution of our code.

4. **Error**: These events indicate that something has gone wrong. The **Source** and **Message** events will usually provide clues as to what has happened.

5. **Fatal**: These events indicate that a fatal error has occurred, and the game can no longer execute.

Your cursor over each of the buttons is indicated in the following screenshot (to be found at the top-right corner of the **Log Viewer** window):

The first five color-coded circles enable us to toggle the different types of events to on or off. They occur in the same order that we examined earlier, beginning with **Debug** and ending with **Fatal**. When your game code is executing, the sheer volume of information being presented through the **Log Viewer** can be overwhelming, and hence, difficult to process mentally. Use these buttons to filter the displayed events, thus making it easier to read/debug.

The next three buttons relate to highlighting significant events for later consideration. The first one is the **Marker**. Simply select an event from the list, and click on this button to mark it. When you have marked multiple events, you can use the next two buttons to move up and down the individual items in your selection of events. The last button, in the form of a red **X**, will clear all of the current events.

You can experiment with the features of the **Log Viewer** discussed earlier, including the filtering options and marking tools. Take some time to absorb the basic purpose of each event type (or event level). Becoming comfortable with all these fundamentals now will speed up our progress throughout the chapters that follow.

Summary

In this chapter, we familiarized ourselves with the non-standard, yet beautiful and intuitive interface of Stencyl. Together, we examined many of the most important areas and views in the Stencyl toolset, including the **Welcome Center**, **Dashboard**, **Scene Designer**, and **Log Viewer**. Having acquired a basic understanding of the structure and layout of Stencyl, we are now ready to begin our fast-paced development project, the completion of which will lead to our mastery of the software. Let's begin – see you in *Chapter 2*, *Starting the Game Project*!

2
Starting the Game Project

As one well-known adage goes, the best way to learn is by doing. In line with that simple truth, every chapter from this point forward will build on a project that we will establish here. The concept, as outlined below, is based on a prototype version of a successful multi-platform game called **Mudslide Cowboy**, developed and published by CyberMyth Games. We will use this chapter to:

- Establish the basics of the control system
- Pinpoint the target gameplay elements
- Outline the core mechanics required to implement the game concepts
- Briefly examine the implied narrative

All of the core, functional features will subsequently be implemented in the following chapters of this book. The original game reached the top eight new games slot in a major European country, and received largely positive player reviews, with an average rating of 4 stars out of 5 on Google Play.

Mudslide Cowboy

Before we attempt to build any game, whether we are using Stencyl or some other game-creation software, it is important to always have at least a basic design brief to work off. I refer here to the concept of a design document. While we do not have the latitude here to present the compilation process for an entire design document, which would be, at the very least, many dozens of pages long — we can and will break down the core concept of the game prototype we will be developing.

The fictional element

Fundamentally, in terms of the fictional element of the game, Mudslide Cowboy is about a cowboy riding a log down a mountain that is prone to landslides. As he rides down the mountain, he must collect coins and treasure, save trapped pilgrims, and dodge bombs being thrown at him from above by his air balloon-riding arch nemesis, Dastardly Dan. It is a relatively simple narrative with the central story arc orbiting around the eventual rescue of Lady Jane, the obligatory love interest. You've got to have one!

The game rules

Gravity pulls the **Player Character** (**PC**) down the mountain, so the player must guide him away from the various obstacles in his path. While paying homage to the always-running game genre (Temple Run, Angry Granny, Chicken Ninja, and so on), the gameplay here is more based on the skills required to juggle multiple mechanics within the game. The player must gather a certain quota of coins to pass the level, but he must also keep the PC alive by not allowing him to collide with cliffs, bombs, boulders, and so on. By the end of the book, you will have created a game demo that looks something like the following screenshot:

As you can see from the preceding screenshot, there are various variables, mechanics, and actors at play and interacting with each other within the constraints of the game world at the same time. By learning to implement all of these, you will gain mastery of the fundamentals of game creation with Stencyl.

Target platforms

This game has been designed specifically to lend itself to both mouse and touch interaction. Therefore, the core game system, with just some small adjustments for each platform, such as ad implementation and certificates, can be built and published to Mac, Windows, PC, IOS, and Android. In practice, we (CyberMyth Games) published the full game to Windows (Desura and IndieCity) and Android (Google Play and Samsung Apps).

As independent game developers, one of the major challenges we face is that of maximizing the audience that receives our game, without greatly increasing the time investment required. Therefore, being able to publish to multiple platforms from one project with few changes is a huge boon. Keep this in mind when you design your games. Use control systems that are easily implemented both on desktop and mobile devices wherever possible.

The control system

Without exception, all the interaction with the game from the player takes place through the mouse or through touch on mobile targets. Hence, we must write our code in such a way that it will determine, using the conditional logic, what a particular click means based on a variety of variables, such as where the cursor is on the screen, whether or not it is over an actor of a certain type, and so on.

Adaptive cursor

The adaptive cursor changes its animation based on the current game state to reflect the player's actions, as shown in the following:

The various possible states are, as seen in the previous screenshot from left to right, as follows:

- **Down**: In this state, the PC is moving directly down the screen
- **Left**: In this state, the PC is veering to the left
- **Right**: In this state, the PC is veering to the right
- **Lasso**: In this state, the player has clicked on a trapped pilgrim and is lassoing him to safety
- **Whip**: In this state, the player has clicked on an obstacle and is whipping it away

The project files

The project files can be downloaded from the Packt Publishing website at (`https://www.packtpub.com/books/content/support`). They come in a ZIP file called `Game Assets`. Extract them to a folder you can easily access, as you will be accessing these files frequently from this point forward. You can download **jZip** for Windows from `http://www.jzip.com` for free if you do not currently have a ZIP extraction program installed on your computer. iZip for Mac should also do the job. Once you have done this, we will begin by creating the stub of our game project.

Creating the game project

Once you open up Stencyl, you will be presented with the **Welcome Center** screen, which is the default opening screen. You should not be inside an opened game. If you are, navigate to **File | Close Game**. Now, on the Dashboard, under **My Projects**, select **Games**, as shown in the following screenshot:

In the main pane, where you are presented with a list of the games currently available in your local installation of Stencyl, you will see a cutout that says **Click here to create new Game** at the very end of the list of games, as shown in the following screenshot:

Click on the aforementioned button, and after a moment, you will be presented with the following window, titled **Create a New Game...**:

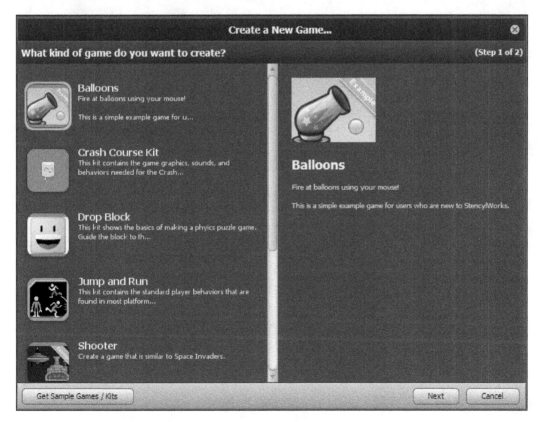

Depending on the version of Stencyl you have installed, you may or may not see a list of game templates, as seen in the preceding screenshot. Scroll down to the bottom of the template list until you see the **Blank Game** button, as shown in the following screenshot:

Select this option, then click on **Next**, and you will be presented with the following window:

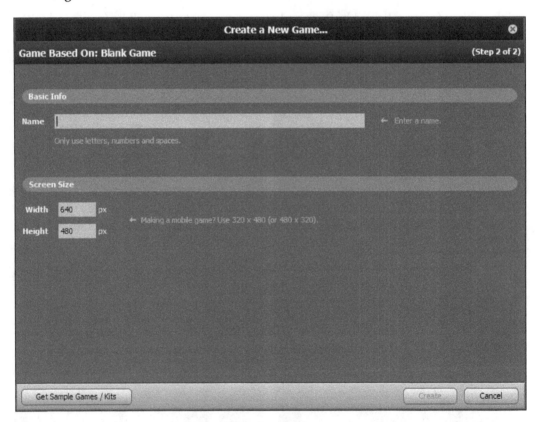

Choose a name for our project; you could simply use the name "Mudslide Cowboy Demo" or something to that effect. Set the **Width** to 480 and **Height** to 720. Once the three fields have been filled in, click on **Create** (which won't be available to click without entering the **Width** and **Height** values), and Stencyl opens the newly created game!

Summary

In this chapter, we established the fundamental concepts for our game project, including details, such as target platform(s), control systems, genre(s), and so on. We also downloaded the game assets folder from the Packt Publishing website, extracted the contents of the ZIP file, and created our first blank game in Stencyl. In the next chapter, we'll start constructing the space of our game, principally through the use of backgrounds and tilesets. In other words, this is where we will begin building worlds, so let's get started!

3

Backgrounds and Tilesets

Backgrounds and tilesets are the two most important asset types in Stencyl when it comes to constructing the ludic (game) and aesthetic aspects of the spaces in our levels. Backgrounds can be used to great effect in providing a fictional context and can assist in creating a sense of depth through the use of effects, such as parallax scrolling, and so on. Tilesets can be used to create a vivid and varied, yet memory-efficient, ludic space within our game levels. In this chapter, we will learn how to:

- Correctly import these two important resource types
- Implement them within our games

 The term ludic is an adjective that means *pertaining to games or play*. It is used in the games industry and is very widely used in academia (game studies). It would be advisable for you to take a moment to absorb its meaning, and assimilate it into your game development vocabulary.

Backgrounds and foregrounds

While the asset type is referred to as a **Background** in Stencyl, they can be used as either backgrounds or foregrounds within our game levels, which means that we can place them either behind or in front of the active play area of our game. In particular, in the case of platform games, the use of both foregrounds and backgrounds with staggered parallax scrolling speeds can create a real sense of richness and depth in our game worlds.

Adding our first background

If the empty game project, we created at the end of *Chapter 2, Starting the Game Project*, is not open on your computer, please reopen it now. On the **Dashboard**, on the left-hand pane with the list of available asset types, click on **Backgrounds**. You should see the following screenshot:

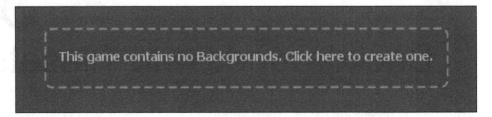

Click on it, and you will be presented with the following window:

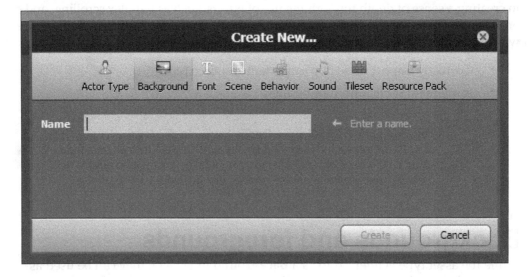

Provide a **Name** for your new background. As a general principle, it is best to be as descriptive as possible at this point so that it is easier to distinguish between our various background assets later on, when we have imported several assets. Perform the following steps:

1. The first background that we are going to import is a grass background, so we'll name this one `Grass Background`.

2. Once you've provided a name, the grayed-out **Create** button shown in the preceding screenshot will become active.

3. Click on it to go to the next screen. After a moment, you should see the following screen open up:

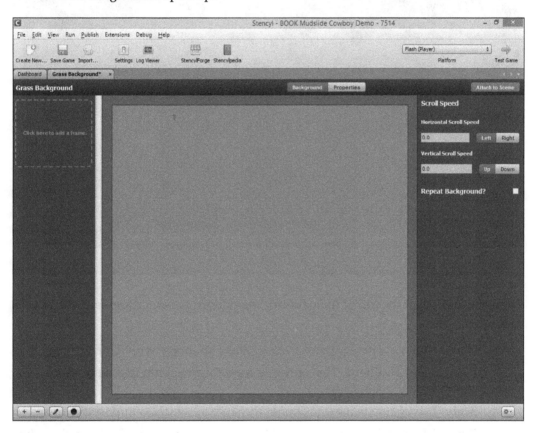

This is the Background Editor. To the right, you will see a pane with various parameters that can be used to create parallax scrolling effects. To the left, we have a button that can be used to add new frames to our background. We can add more than one frame if we wish to animate the background, though excessive use of this feature is likely to adversely impact memory and performance, especially on mobile targets. Click on the **Add Frame** button, and you will be presented with the following window:

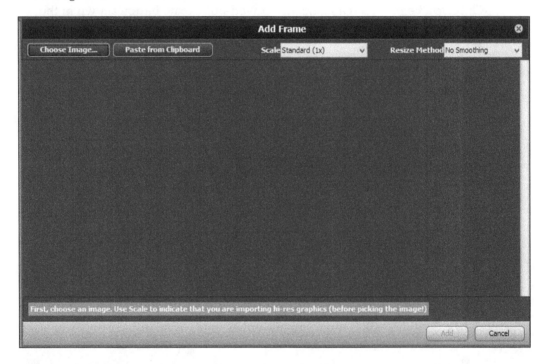

From left to right, at the top of the window, the options we are presented with are as follows:

- **Choose Image**: This option is used to select an image with a file browser
- **Paste from Clipboard**: This option is used to paste bitmap data from the clipboard into the frame
- **Scale**: This option is used to choose the scale at which to import the image
- **Resize Method**: This option is used to choose your preferred resizing algorithm

Before clicking on the **Choose Image** button, we must first ensure that we have selected the correct **Scale** and **Resize Method** (or algorithm), and configure a few other settings. Follow these steps:

1. First, set the **Resize Method** to **Bicubic** if this is not already the setting. Our game graphics have all been created at **4X** scale, the highest resolution available. This caters for all targets, irrespective of screen dimensions or resolution. Stencyl will generate the lower resolution versions of the images (1X, 2X) automatically from the 4X version we provide.

2. Select **4X** from the drop-down menu, then click on the **Choose Image** button. This will open a file explorer.

3. Simply navigate to the directory where you extracted the contents of the game assets ZIP file we downloaded in the previous chapter. Navigate to Game Assets | Graphics | Backgrounds and import Grass Background. png, as shown in the following screenshot:

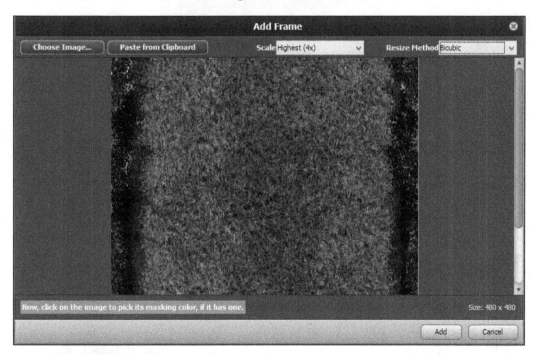

Click on the **Add** button at the bottom-right corner of the window, and you will have imported your first static background into Stencyl. Congratulations! Next, we want to configure our parallax scrolling settings for the background:

1. You can tick the **Repeat Background** checkbox seen in the following screenshot:

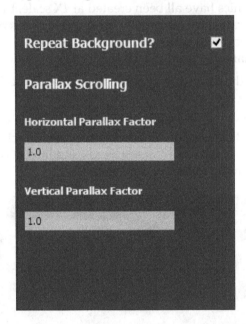

2. This will open up the **Parallax Scrolling** options.

3. The current setting for **Horizontal** and **Vertical Parallax Factor** are 1.0 by default. For this background, that is appropriate, so we will leave these settings unchanged.

Three more backgrounds

Now, let's test what we learned so far. Let's repeat the steps we just followed to import the following three background images found in the same **Backgrounds** directory as the first image we imported:

- `Home Screen Background`: This background image uses the exact same settings as before

- `Plain Wood Background`: This background image uses the exact same settings as before

- `Bushy Foreground`: For this background, we need to change the vertical parallax factor to 1.2

Well done! We have successfully imported and configured all of the background images needed to build our prototype game. Now we just need to import our first tileset, and we can start building our own 2D game worlds!

Our first tileset

A tileset is a collection of reusable tiles that we can use to create complex and varied level geometry with marginal impact on file size and memory consumption, when compared with the equivalent impact that would be incurred were we to custom paint every detail of our levels without the use of such repeatable units. At **1X** scale, the tiles in our tileset are 32 by 32 pixels; at **4X** scale, they are 128 by 128 pixels. As with all of our graphical assets, we will be importing our tileset at **4X** scale, allowing Stencyl to automatically generate all of the other scales.

Let's bring the tileset into our game. The process is not dissimilar to the steps we followed when importing the backgrounds earlier.

Go to the **Dashboard**, and select **Tilesets** from the list of **RESOURCES** in the left-hand pane. Click on the **This game contains no Tilesets. Click here to create one** button, and you'll be prompted to provide a **name**. Name it Green Tileset, and click on **Create**. You will see the following window. Do not click on anything as yet:

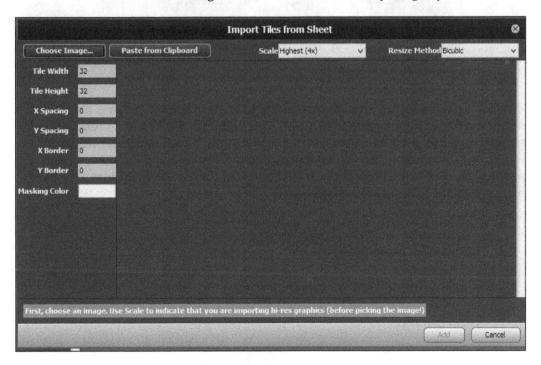

Click on **Choose Image**, and the file browser will open, as it did during the importing process for our backgrounds. Navigate to the game assets folder as before. The tileset can be found in the Game Assets/Graphics/Tilesets/green grass tileset.png directory. If successful, you should see the tileset fill the window like the following screenshot:

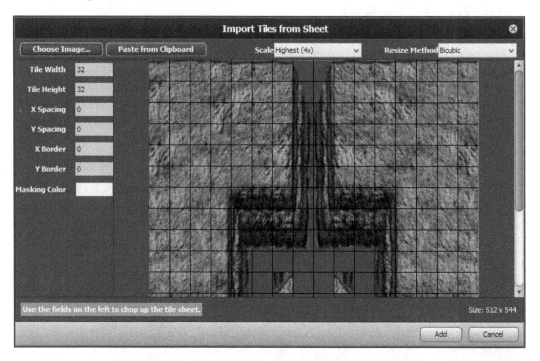

When working in Stencyl, we always see the 1X scale graphics, as this is the default resolution for desktop targets (Windows, Mac, and Linux). The higher resolution graphics are only used when we test or run the game. Which particular resolution is utilized at runtime depends on the platform and device being targeted, screen dimensions, and so on. Now click on an individual tile to edit its settings. The two most important settings to be configured are as follows:

- **Collision Bounds**: Here, we can set either a box or polygonal collision shape for the various tiles in our tileset by clicking on the required shape, as shown in the panel. If the tile is blank, or if it's a tile that actors should be able to pass through, we must set it to **No Collisions**, which is the top-left option in the collision bounds shapes window. All the tiles are set to the square collision shape by default and must be altered if this does not fit the particular tile.

- **Frames**: By default, all the tiles have just one frame — most tiles are static. If you wish to animate a tile (water, lava, and so on), you can import additional frames and set their duration in milliseconds, as shown in the following screenshot:

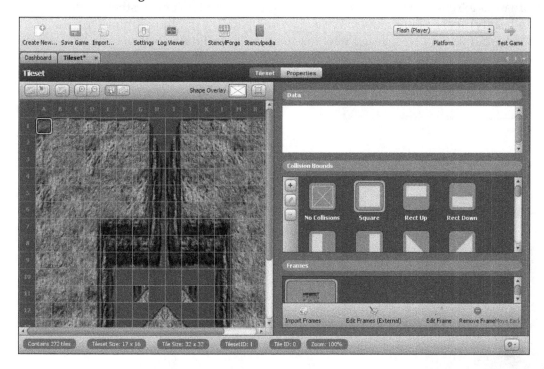

 If you click and drag the tilesheet from one tile location to another, you can make a rectangular selection of multiple tiles. This can be timesaving if you wish to set the same collision shape for multiple tiles. Try it.

Each tile in the set has its own collision bound, highlighted in the **Collision Bounds** pane to the right. Be sure to match the **Collision Bounds** pane to the visible part of the tile as closely as possible, using the various shapes available under **Collision Bounds** to the right of the screen. You can create custom shapes, if you want to be very precise, by clicking on the plus (**+**) button at the top left of the **Collision Bounds** window, as shown in the preceding screenshot. When you are satisfied, save your progress, and click on the close (**x**) icon on the **Tileset** tab, which is to the right of the **Dashboard** tab toward the top of the screen, to close out the editor for now.

Summary

In this chapter, we learned the processes involved in importing two of the most significant graphical resource types in Stencyl: **Backgrounds** and **Tilesets**, which are used to sculpt the ludic (pertaining to games and play) and aesthetic (pertaining to beauty) space of our games. We configured parallax scrolling settings for our backgrounds, and we learned how to cater for all resolutions by importing at 4X scale and allowing Stencyl to generate the lower resolutions using a bicubic algorithm. In the next chapter, we'll learn how to use these newly imported game assets to start building out the space of our game levels!

4

Building Levels Using Scenes

So far, we learned how to freely navigate to the various parts of the Stencyl interface, establish a clear concept for our game project, create **Backgrounds** and **Tilesets**, and configure these game resources so that they are ready for use within our game levels. How do we build the levels themselves? In this chapter, we will learn how to:

- Use scenes to construct the first level for our game
- Attach backgrounds and foregrounds to the scene
- Sculpt level geometry through the intelligent use of the tileset
- Toggle background and foreground rendering on and off

Creating our first level

If you have not already done so, please open the game project in Stencyl. On the **Dashboard**, under the list of **RESOURCES** in the left-hand pane, click on **Scenes**.

You will see that the game currently contains no scenes, as shown in the following screenshot:

Click on **This game contains no Scenes. Click here to create one** to create the first level. We will be presented with a window where we are required to provide configuration data before we proceed with Stencyl. You should see the following window, without the **Name**, which I have provided for you to copy:

Let's proceed with the initial configuration of the scene by filling in the following fields:

- **Name**: We can name the scene Level 1, as shown in the previous screenshot. We will follow this convention for the naming of all our levels, so the second level will be Level 2 and so on.

- **Width**: By default, the scene width is measured in tiles. It is currently set to be the same width as the game window. We will not change this setting, as it fits our game design perfectly.

- **Height**: The scene height is also measured in tiles. Let's set this to 100 for now.

- **Tile Width, Tile Height**: Our tiles are 32 by 32; hence, do not alter these settings.

- **Background Color**: We can provide either a single background color or a gradient. This option is only relevant for levels that do not have background images. Ours will have a background, so let's leave this setting alone.

- **Create**: Click on the **Create** button to proceed to the next screen.

Implementing foregrounds and backgrounds

To implement foregrounds and backgrounds, perform the following steps:

1. To implement foregrounds and backgrounds within our scene, we must click on the **+** button at the bottom-left section of the **Layers** pane as shown in the following screenshot, and select **New Background Layer**:

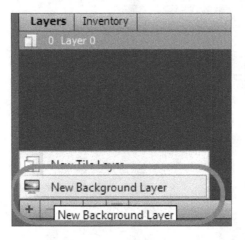

2. You will be presented with the following **Choose a Background** window:

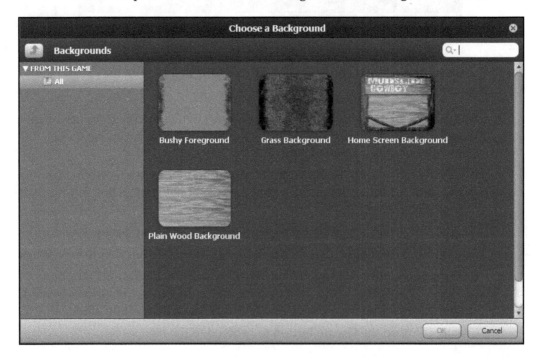

3. Choose **Grass Background**, which is the second option displayed in the list of available backgrounds, as shown in the previous screenshot.

4. Now click on **OK**, and you will see that an item has been added to the list of **Layers** attached to the scene, and the main view has been filled with the **1x** graphic of the background we just imported.

5. This is a background image, which is rendered at the top of the layer stack; however, click on the **Send Layer Back** button to move it to the bottom, where it belongs, as shown in the following screenshot:

6. Click on the **+** button again in the **Layers** pane to add another background layer in the same manner as before. This time, select the **Bushy Foreground**, which happens to be the first option that appears in the list:

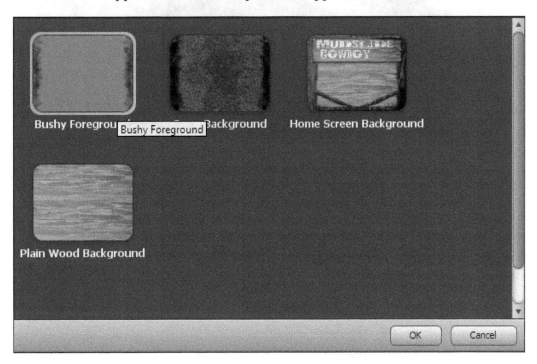

At this point, you should see the foreground and background rendering of the scene display as follows:

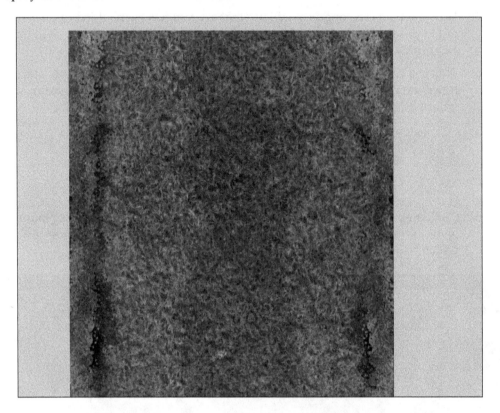

If you scroll up and down the scene, you will see that both the foreground and background repeat seamlessly on the y-axis, enabling us to create game levels that are as large or as small as we may prefer. The seam between the top and bottom has intentionally been painted in a graphics editor to facilitate this. If either of the backgrounds in use are not repeating vertically, as expected, open up the **Background** and make sure the **Repeat Background** option is ticked.

Adding tiles to our level

Let's take a look at the **Palette** option on the right-hand side of the screen, and you will see that the tiles that we imported in *Chapter 3, Backgrounds and Tilesets,* are now available for use within the scene, as shown in the following screenshot:

Notice that the top-left tile is highlighted with a yellow border. This indicates that it is the currently selected tile. You can create larger, rectangular selections of tiles by performing the following steps:

1. Click on the top-left tile.
2. Drag it to the bottom-right tile of your choice.
3. Release the left mouse button.

Make the following selection of tiles, as shown in the following screenshot:

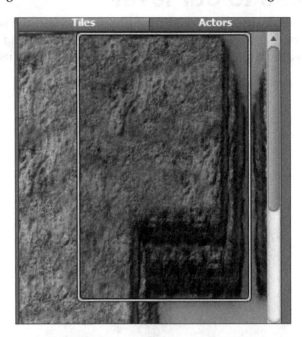

Select **Layer 0**, which is a tiles layer (tiles cannot be added to the background layers), and with these tiles selected, move the mouse over to the top-left corner of the scene, and then click once to place them in the top-left corner, as shown in the following screenshot:

Congratulations! You've just placed the first few tiles of your very first game level! Let's build on this. Select the connecting tiles below the previous selection, as shown in the following screenshot:

Now, click once to place them below the existing tiles so that they continue the functional and aesthetic flow of the level. Stack the same group of tiles three times vertically to get more distance out of them. Then, go back to the tileset, and select the symmetrical tiles on the right-hand side of the tileset. Use them to mirror what you have already created on the left-hand side of the level. What you create should look the same as, or similar to, what you see in the following screenshot:

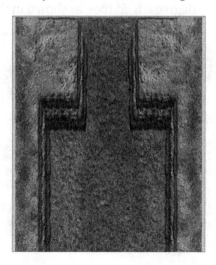

Let's add a little variety to the style and shape of our terrain. Perform the following steps to do so:

1. Select the tile shown in the following screenshot:

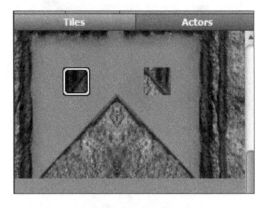

2. Place it as shown in the following screenshot (I've toggled the background and foreground display off so that it is easier to discern exactly where the tiles are being placed):

3. Next, select these 45-degree edged tiles, as shown in the following screenshot:

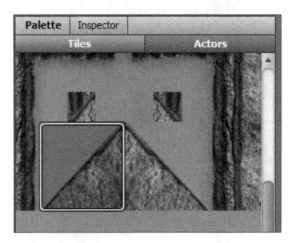

4. Place them on the level and be sure to align them in order to create the intended visual effect, as shown in the following screenshot:

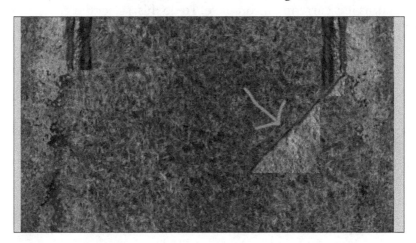

5. Sometimes, as a byproduct of placing a group of tiles at the same time, we can end up adding blank tiles as well. In this particular case, there are three culprits; all at the top-left corner of the tile group we just placed. Their exact positions are shown in the following screenshot. Select them and press the *Delete* key on your keyboard:

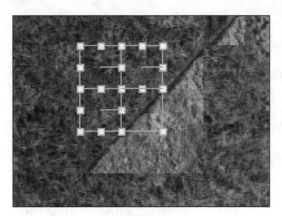

6. Having cleared away the unwanted blank tiles, our final step in this tile-based part of the lesson will be to finish off our section of 45-degree terrain, as it is currently incomplete. To do this, select the group of tiles shown in the following screenshot:

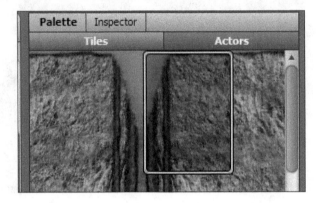

7. Next, place them at the base of the 45-degree tiles that we added previously:

Excellent work! You've successfully created some tile-based geometry in your game. Tiles can be used to create a great variety in the aesthetic and ludic space of your game with minimum impact on memory or performance due to their efficient nature. Although it is not suitable for this particular tileset, in many cases, you can select a tile, then click and drag from one location to another in the scene view to paint multiple copies of that tile, which can be a speedy way of blocking out the space of your levels!

Exercise

Let's put these newfound level design skills into practice! Using the various tiles in the tileset, keep working on the tile arrangement in the level until you achieve something that blends aesthetically like the following screenshot:

When you have accomplished this, continue to fill out the level with these tile groups until you have the full **100** vertical rows sculpted (23 of which are shown in the previous screenshot). Use artistic license here. I want you to make this level your own. One principle to keep in mind while you're doing this is to be sure that there is always a channel somewhere in the layout of the level that allows the player character to continue moving downwards. Stagger the layout of these channels to add an element of challenge for the player. Congratulations! You have completed your first tile-based level.

Summary

In this chapter, we learned how to utilize backgrounds, foregrounds, and tiles to sculpt a visually compelling and varied level. We learned how to add tiles individually and in groups, and remove those that were accidentally placed or no longer wanted. There is still a notable absence of action in the game, however, as we have yet to add any actors into the mix. Working with actors to populate our levels will be the subject of the next chapter.

5
Actor Types and Instances

So far, we have come quite a long way in terms of assimilating the essential Stencyl workflow and learning how to structure the levels in our games, including the implementation of foregrounds, backgrounds, and tilesets to create ludic spaces. However, it is impossible to implement the actual gameplay elements without first learning how to create and deploy Actors in our levels. In this chapter, we will cover all the fundamentals of working with Actor types and instances. The key points covered here will include:

- Creating **Actor Types**
- Importing **Animations**
- Customizing **Animations**, including frame duration in milliseconds and so on
- Editing physics settings, such as, but not limited to, mass, linear and angular drag, friction, and bounce
- Customizing collision shapes
- Adding **Actor** instances to our **Scenes** and customizing them if required

By the end of this chapter, you will have the ability to implement the core gameplay elements into your games through the effective utilization of **Actors**. This will be further built upon in subsequent chapters, where we will examine the process of building basic and advanced **Behaviors** from scratch using Stencyl's signature visual programming interface.

What are actors?

In Stencyl, only two resource types can have **Behaviors** or code attached to them. The relevant **Behavior** types are as follows:

- **Scene Behaviors**: These are attached to **Scenes** and are usually used to handle more global events, such as timers and score keeping, not specific to one actor

- **Actor Behaviors**: These are attached to **Actors** themselves and are generally used to govern their movement around the level, their physical interaction with other actors or tiles, and in some cases, to make the actor respond to user input

Coupling **Actors** with **Actor Behaviors** in an intelligent fashion allows us to create an unlimited variety of game mechanics and gameplay elements. Hence, the creative use of **Actors** is the key to bringing our game concepts to life within Stencyl.

Adding our first actor

Let's begin by adding the avatar, which will symbolize the player in the game, in game development parlance. The actor that represents the player in-game is generally referred to by the acronym **PC (Player Character)**. Having established this, we will use this abbreviation from time to time henceforth. Perform the following steps for adding our first actor:

1. Go to the **Dashboard**, and take a look at the now familiar **RESOURCES** pane on the left-hand side of the screen. Select **Actor Types**, which just so happens to be at the top of the list, as shown in the following screenshot:

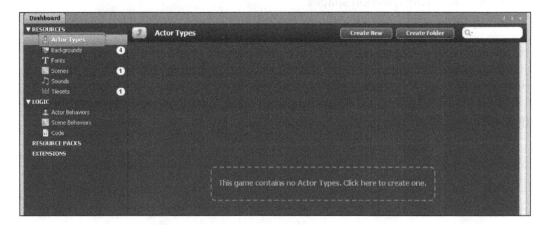

2. You can see that there is a cut-out styled button in the main view that contains the text **This game contains no Actor Types. Click here to create one.** Do as it says, and the **Create New...** window will pop up, as shown in the following screenshot. We are not complete strangers to this window, as it is the same window we used to create our **Backgrounds**, foreground, and **Tilesets** in *Chapter 3, Backgrounds and Tilesets*. We must provide a name next to the **Name** box to proceed to the **Actor Type Editor**. Let's simply call this actor Cowboy:

3. Click on **Create**. The **Actor Type** editor will now open up. What you should see is a screen as shown in the following screenshot:

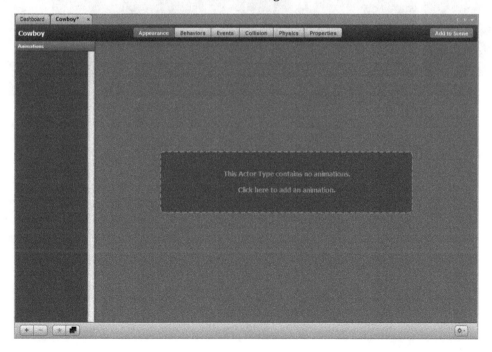

Importing our first animation

One of the first things that we'll need to do, now that we've created the shell of our **Actor Type**, is import a few animations so that the actor has a visual representation within the game. Perform the following steps:

1. You should see the **This Actor Type contains no animations. Click here to add an animation.** button at the center of the main view, as shown in the preceding screenshot. Click on it to add the first animation. You will be presented with a blank animation called **Animation 0**, as shown in the following screenshot:

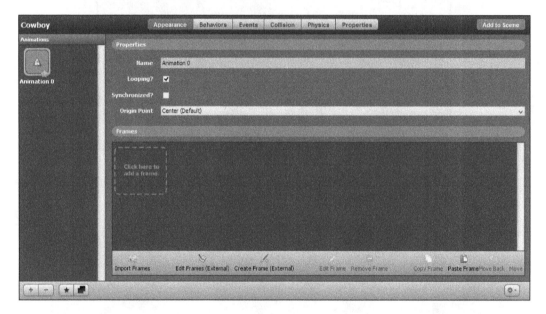

2. In the main view, under **Frames**, you will see a **Click here to add a frame.** button. Click on it, and the **Import Frames from Image Strip** window will pop up, as shown in the following screenshot:

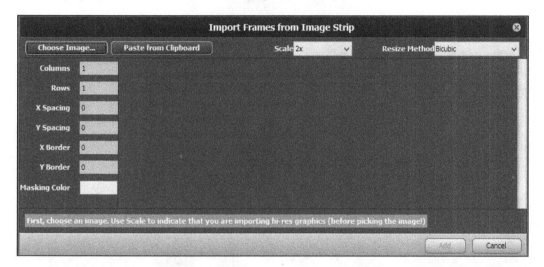

3. Change **Scale** to **4x**, as we did in *Chapter 3, Backgrounds and Tilesets*, when importing the graphics for the **Backgrounds** and **Tilesets** game resources. It is important that we always do this, lest our graphics import at incorrect scales.

4. Now click on **Choose Image...** to open the file explorer.

5. Navigate to and select Game Assets/Graphics/Actor Animations/cowboy down.png.

Having completed the preceding steps, you should now be able to see the selected graphic appear in the **Import Frames from Image Strip** window, as shown in the following screenshot:

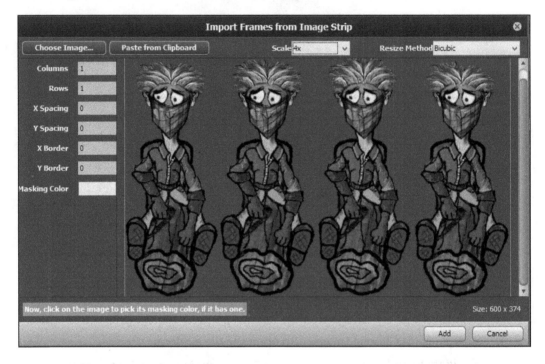

Clearly, this animation contains four horizontal frames. Hence, before clicking on **Add**, we must perform the following steps:

1. Change **Columns** to 4.
2. Leave all of the other fields unaltered, and click on **Add**.

3. You will see that we have successfully added our first animation. Well done! At this point, it is important to change the name of the animation to something more meaningful. The **Animation 0** name doesn't say much about the aesthetic or functional role of the animation. Change the **Name** to Down, as shown in the following screenshot:

The other fields, **Looping**, **Synchronized**, and **Origin Point** are ideally configured by default in this case, so we need not change them. We have two more animations to import for this **Actor**. On the left-hand side of the screen, at the bottom of the **Animations** pane, you will see a number of buttons, as shown in the following screenshot:

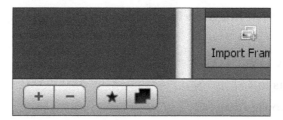

The names of these buttons appear on the screen when you hover the mouse cursor over them. These are, from left to right, as follows:

- **Create Animation**: This button adds a new animation to this **Actor Type**
- **Remove Animation**: This button removes the selected animation from this **Actor Type**
- **Set as Default Animation**: This button makes the selected animation the default animation
- **Duplicate Animation**: This button duplicates the selected animation

Now let's click on the **Create Animation** button to add our second animation. You will see, as shown in the following screenshot, that there are now two animations in our **Animations** pane. The new animation is called **Animation 1** and is still blank, as we have not yet imported the frame sheet. Change the **Name** to Left, and select the **Click here to add a frame.** button, as shown at the bottom center of the following screenshot:

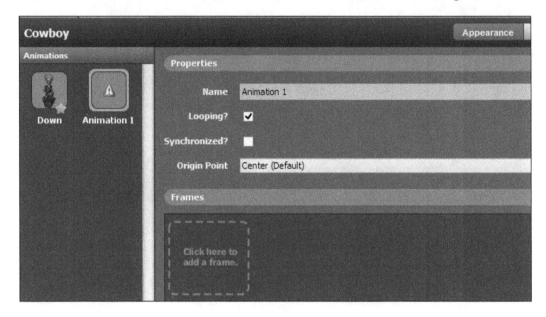

The **Import Frames from Image Strip** window will open once again. Perform the following steps:

1. Set the **Scale** to **4x**.

2. Set **Columns** to 4.

3. Click on **Choose Image...**.

4. Navigate to and select Game Assets\Graphics\Actor Animations\cowboy left.png.

5. Click on **Add**.

If you have followed the steps correctly, you should see something like the following screenshot:

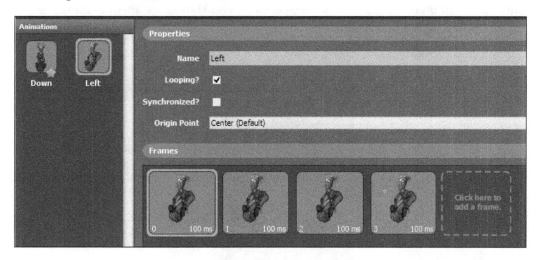

If this is not what you see, click on the **Remove Animation** button (alternatively, you can select the **Left** animation in the **Animations** pane, and press *Delete* on your keyboard), and repeat the aforementioned steps carefully so that you can achieve the desired result.

We have one more animation to import for this actor. Let's follow all the same steps as follows:

1. Click on **Create Animation**.
2. Change the new animation's **Name** to Right.
3. Select the **Click here to add a frame.** button.
4. The **Import Frames from Image Strip** window appears. Change **Scale** to 4x, and **Columns** to 4.
5. Click on the **Choose Image...** button.
6. Navigate to and select Game Assets/Graphics/Actor Animations/cowboy right.png.
7. Click on **Add**.

As mentioned earlier, if you have followed the steps correctly, you should see three functional animations looping in the **Animations** pane at this point (the animations are subtle, but if you take a look at them closely, you should see them looping), as shown in the following screenshot:

You will notice that one of the animations (**Down**) has a star on it. This indicates that it is the default animation. If any or all of these animations are not looping, make sure that you have checked the **Looping** checkbox for each individual animation (it is usually checked by default), as shown in the following screenshot:

Collision shapes

Each animation has its own collision shape, so it's important to take a little time to configure this properly. We'll start by selecting the **Down** animation from the **Animations** pane, then switching to the **Collision** context. Take a look at the options shown in the following screenshot:

You will see that, by default, your actor has a collision box, which encompasses the entirety of the graphic, as shown in the following screenshot:

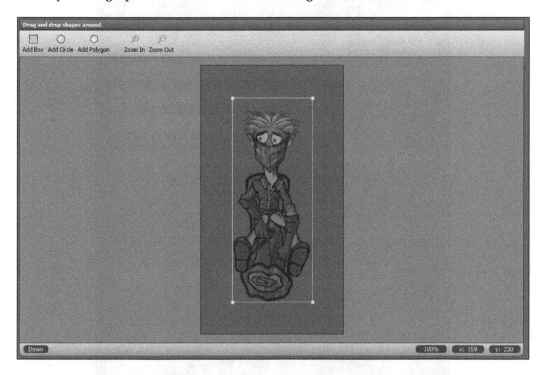

While we do want to use a box-shaped collision for this particular animation, we must customize its position and its dimensions to fit a certain area of the graphic. At the top right of the screen, you will see a pane called **Current Shape**.

Take a look at the following screenshot:

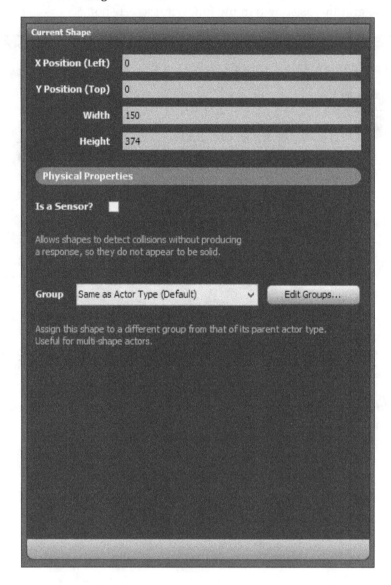

Let's alter the following values to better suit this animation:

1. Set **X Position (Left)** to 18.

2. Set **Y Position (Top)** to 68.

3. Set **Width** to 34.

4. Set **Height** to 90.

You should now be able to see the updated collision shape to fit the desired collision area on our **Animation** preview:

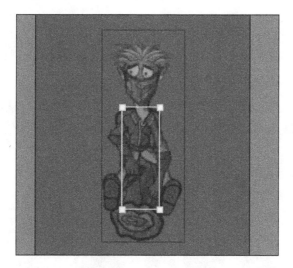

Excellent work! You have successfully configured the collision settings for your first animation. Let's get started with the other two animations. In the **Animation** pane on the left-hand side of the screen, switch to the **Left** animation. You will see a box collision shape, which encompasses the entire graphic, as before. This time, you must perform the following steps:

1. Select the collision box.

2. Press the *Delete* key on your keyboard.

We are going to add a polygonal collision shape to this animation. Click on the **Add Polygon** button shown in the following screenshot:

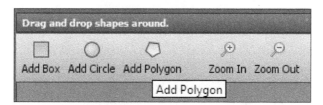

The **Create a Polygon...** window will appear on the screen as shown in the following screenshot:

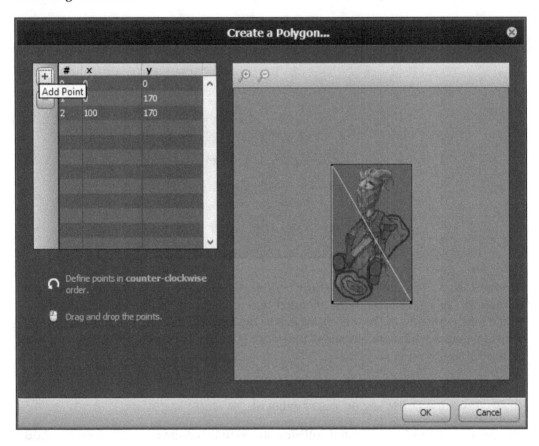

This polygon has only three points by default. We need four to create the intended shape, so let's add an extra point. Click on the **Add Point** button at the top-left section of the window (it looks like a plus symbol). You should see an additional point appear in the preview on the right-hand side of the window. Finally, let's move the points around to create the shape, as shown in the following screenshot, simply by clicking-and-dragging them around in the preview. The goal here is to approximate the visual area of the log (be aware that the concave collision shapes are prohibited and will not be accepted), as shown in the following screenshot:

When you have succeeded in creating this shape, click on **OK** to commit and add this shape to the animation. Now, we must create the inverse shape for the **Right** animation:

1. Select the **Right** animation from the **Animations** pane on the left-hand side of the screen.

2. Select the existing collision box shape and press *Delete* on your keyboard to get rid of it.

3. Click on **Add Polygon** to open the **Create a Polygon...** window.

4. Click on **Add Point** (which looks like a plus symbol) to increase the number of points from three to four.

5. Manipulate the positions of each point by clicking and dragging them in the preview, until you have a shape that looks the same as or very similar to the following screenshot:

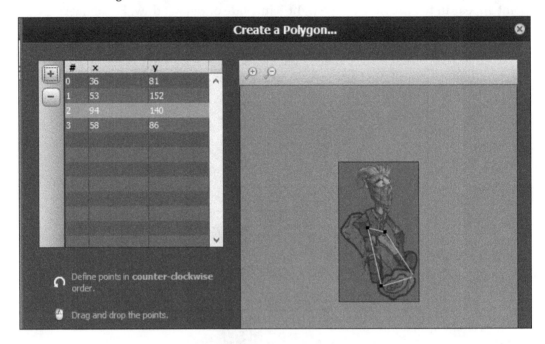

6. Click on **OK** to commit this collision shape to the animation.

Congratulations! You've successfully added both the basic and advanced collision shapes to your animations! Now, we just need to finalize some of the **Physics** settings for this **Actor Type**. Switch to the **Physics** context, as shown in the following screenshot:

Under the **General** settings, you will see the following options:

- Set **What kind of Actor Type?** to **Normal**
- Set **Can Rotate?** to **No**
- Set **Affected by Gravity?** to **Yes**

Take a look at the following screenshot that shows the options shown in the **General** settings:

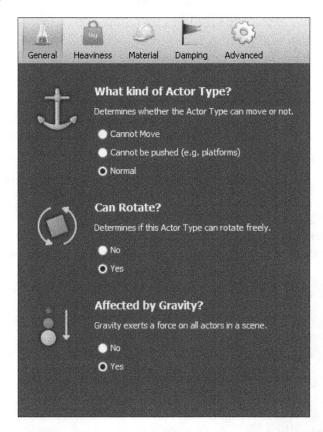

Well done! You've successfully configured all of the fundamental settings for the **Cowboy** actor! This **Actor Type** now has useable animations and is capable of detecting and reacting to the physical interactions within our game levels using **Collision** shapes!

Importing the rock Actor Type

We must add one more actor to our game, which will be easy now that we've learned the process, before moving on to the next chapter, where we'll begin by writing **Behaviors** to make our actors do things in-game. This time, we'll add an obstacle in the form of a falling rock. Perform the following steps:

1. Go back to the **Dashboard**.
2. In the **RESOURCES** menu on the left-hand side of the screen, select **Actor Types**.

3. Click on the button that says **Click here to create a new Actor Type**.

4. Set the **Name** to Rock and then click on **Create**.

5. Click on **This Actor Type contains no animations. Click here to add an animation**.

6. Select the **Click here to add a frame.** button to import our animations using the **Import Frame from Image Strip** window.

7. Set **Scale** to **4x**, then click on **Choose Image…**, and navigate to and select Game Assets\Graphics\Actor Animations\large rock.png. Set **Columns** and **Rows** to 1, **Resize Method** to **Bicubic**, and then click on **Add**.

8. Change the **Name** of the new animation from **Animation 0** to Default.

9. Change the context in the top menu from **Appearance** to **Collision**.

10. Select the default collision box and press *Delete* on the keyboard. Then, click on **Add Circle**, and in the ensuing window, set the fields **X Position (Left)** to 4, **Y Position (Top)** to 0, and **Radius** to 16. Then, click on **OK** to commit this collision shape to the animation, as shown in the following screenshot:

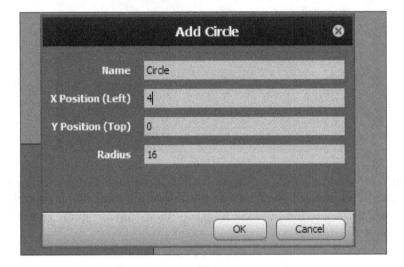

11. Switch back to the **Appearance** context in the top menu, and then select the **Duplicate Animation** button (which looks similar to overlapping squares) at the bottom of the **Animations** window on the left-hand side of the screen.

12. The new animation is named **Animation 1** by default and will have the same collision shape as the animation we copied it from. Duplicating has allowed us to avoid the time-wasting act of recreating it over and over again for each animation. Change the **Name** of this animation to Cracked.

13. Select the **Click here to add a frame.** button. Click on **Choose Image...**, then navigate to and select Game Assets\Graphics\Actor Animations\large rock cracked.png. Click on **Add**.

14. Select the first frame of this animation to appear in the **Frames** pane. This is the leftover from the animation that we copied, and it must be removed. Press *Delete* on the keyboard to remove it (be careful not to delete the second frame by mistake):

15. Select the **Duplicate Animation** button one more time, and this time, change the **Name** of the newly created animation to Exploding.

16. Once more, select the **Click here to add a frame.** button. Click on **Choose Image...**, then navigate to and select Game Assets\Graphics\Actor Animations\large rock exploding.png. Set **Columns** to 3, then click on **Add**.

17. As we did for the previous animation, select the first frame of this animation to appear in the **Frames** pane. This is the leftover from the animation that we just copied, so it must be removed. Press *Delete* on the keyboard to remove it.

What you will now see in the **Animations** pane should be an **Actor Type** with three animations, which is similar to the one shown in the following screenshot:

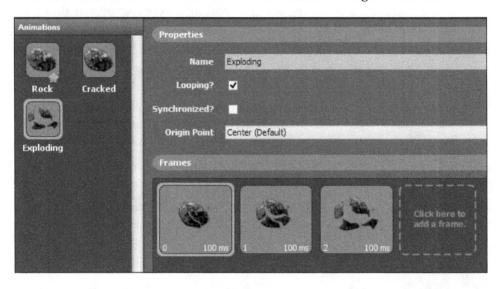

Finally, let's switch our editing context from **Appearance** to **Physics** in the top menu:

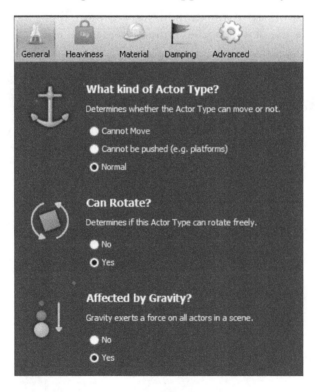

Then, perform the following steps:

1. Set **What kind of Actor Type?** to **Normal**.
2. Set **Can Rotate?** to **Yes**.
3. Set **Affected by Gravity?** to **Yes**.
4. Now, switch from the **General** settings to the **Heaviness** settings.
5. Set **Mass** to 30.
6. Set **Angular Mass** to 60, as shown in the following screenshot:

Summary

Excellent job! You have now successfully created two very important **Actor Types** and configured all of their core settings, including the application of box, circle, and polygon collision shapes. In the next chapter, we will write our first **Actor Behavior**, and use this to control the movement of the **Player Character** (PC) through our levels, cycle, and switch animations, and handle its physical interactions with the other elements of the game world. Let's get going; it's time to start programming some gameplay!

6
Writing Simple Behaviors

In this chapter, we will begin using Stencyl's signature visual programming interface to create logic and interaction in our game. We will create this logic using a **WYSIWYG (What You See Is What You Get)** block-snapping interface. By the end of this chapter, you will have the Player Character whizzing down the screen in pursuit of a zigzagging air balloon! Some of the things we will learn to do in this chapter are as follows:

- Create **Actor Behaviors** and attach them to **Actor Types**
- Add **Events** to our **Behaviors**
- Use **If blocks** to create branching and conditional logic to handle the various states within our game
- Accept and react to the input from the player
- Apply physical forces to **Actors** in real time

One of the great things about this visual approach to programming is that it largely removes the unpleasantness of dealing with the syntax (the rules of the programming language), and the inevitable errors that come with it when we're creating logic for our game. This allows us to focus on the things that matter the most in our games: smooth, well-wrought game mechanics and enjoyable, well-crafted gameplay.

The player handler

The first behavior that we are going to create is the **Player Handler**. This behavior will be attached to the **Player Character (PC)** that exists in the form of the Cowboy Actor Type. This behavior will be used to handle much of the game logic and will process the lion's share of the player input.

Creating a new actor behavior

It's time to create our very first behavior! Go to the **Dashboard**, under the **LOGIC** heading, select **Actor Behaviors**, as shown in the following screenshot:

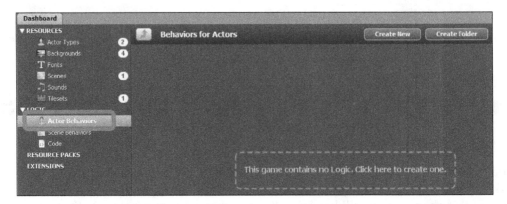

Click on **This game contains no Logic. Click here to create one.** to add your first behavior. You should see the **Create New...** window appear:

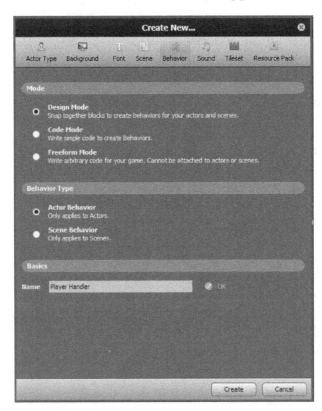

Enter the **Name** as `Player Handler`, as shown in the previous screenshot, then click on **Create**. You will be taken to the behavior designer window, as shown in the following screenshot:

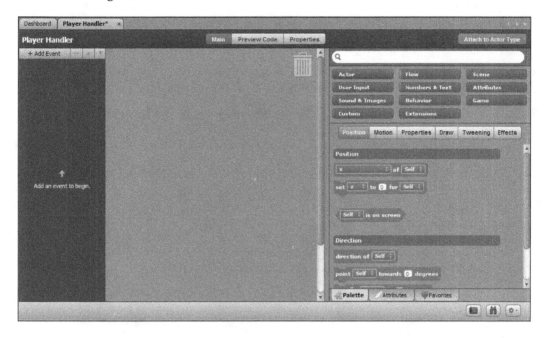

Let's take a moment to examine the various areas within the behavior designer window. From left to right, as shown in the preceding screenshot, we have the following:

- **Events Pane**: In this area, we can add, remove, and move between the events in our behavior.

- **Canvas**: On the center of the screen, the canvas is where we can drag the blocks around in order to click on our game logic together.

- **Blocks Palette**: This is where we can find any and all of the various logic blocks that Stencyl has to offer. Simply navigate to your category of choice, then click and drag the block onto the canvas to configure it.

Perform the following steps:

1. Click on the **Add Event** button, which can be found at the very top of the events pane.

2. In the menu that ensues, go to **Basics** and click on **When Updating**, as shown in the following screenshot:

You will notice that we now have an event in our events pane, called **Updated**, along with a block called **always** on our canvas. In Stencyl events lingo, **always** is synonymous with **When Updating**. Take a look at the following screenshot:

Since this is the only event in our Behavior at this time, it will be selected by default. The **always** block (which is a yellow block with a red flag) is where we will put the game logic that needs to be checked on a constant basis for every update of the game loop (this will be commensurate with the frame rate at runtime, around 60 fps, depending on the game performance and system specs). Before we proceed with the creation of our conditional logic, we must first create a few attributes.

 If you have a programming background, it is easy to understand the attributes as being synonymous with local variables. Just like variables, they have a set data type, and you can retrieve or change the value of an attribute in real time.

Creating attributes

Switch to the **Attributes** context in the blocks palette, as shown in the following screenshot:

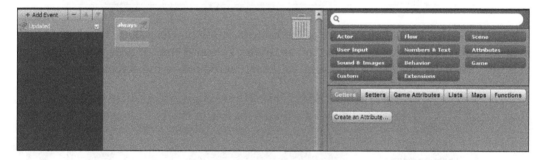

There are currently no attributes associated with this behavior. Let's add some, as we'll need them to store the important information of the various types, which we'll use later on to craft the game mechanics. Click on the **Create an Attribute...** button, as shown in the following screenshot:

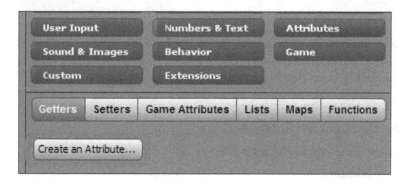

In the **Create an Attribute...** window that appears, enter the **Name** as `Target Actor`, set **Type** to **Actor**, check **Hidden?**, and click on **OK**, as shown in the following screenshot:

Congratulations! If you take a look at the bottom of the blocks palette window, you will see that you have added your first attribute, **Target Actor**, of type **Actor**, and it is now available for use in our code, as shown in the following screenshot:

Next, let's add the five Boolean attributes. A Boolean is a special kind of an attribute that can be set to either true or false. These are the only two values that it can accept. First, let's create the "Can Be Hurt" Boolean, by performing the following steps:

1. Click on **Create an Attribute...**
2. Enter the **Name** as `Can Be Hurt`.
3. Change the **Type** to **Boolean**.
4. Check **Hidden?**

5. Click on **OK** to commit and add the attribute to the behavior.

6. Repeat steps 1 through 5 for the remaining four Boolean attributes to be added, each time substituting the appropriate name with the following:

   ◦ Can Switch Anim

   ◦ Draw Lasso

   ◦ Lasso Back

   ◦ Mouse Over

If you have done this correctly, you should now see six attributes in your attributes list; one under **Actor** and five under **Boolean**, as shown in the following screenshot:

Now let's follow the same process to further create seven attributes, only this time, we'll set the **Type** for all of them to **Number**. The **Name** for each one will be as follows:

- Health (set to **Hidden?**)
- Impact Force (set to **Hidden?**)
- Lasso Distance (set to **Hidden?**)
- Max Health (don't set to **Hidden?**)
- Turn Force (don't set to **Hidden?**)
- X Point (set to **Hidden?**)
- Y Point (set to **Hidden?**)

If all goes well, you should see your list of attributes updated according to the following screenshot:

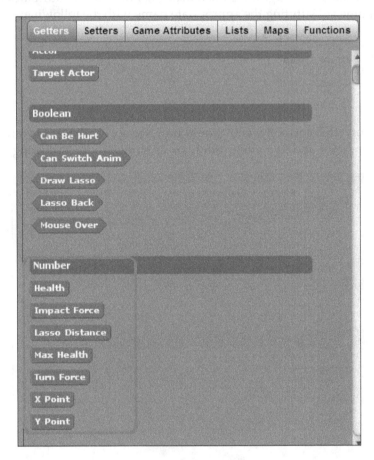

We will add just one additional attribute. Click on the **Create an Attribute...** button again and perform the following steps:

1. Name it Mouse State.
2. Change its **Type** to **Text**.
3. Do not hide this attribute.
4. Click on **OK** to commit and add the attribute to your behavior.

Excellent work! At this point, you have created all of the attributes you will need for the **Player Handler** behavior!

Custom events

We need to create a few custom events in order to complete the code for this game prototype. For programmers, custom events are like functions that don't accept parameters. You simply trigger them at will in order to execute a reusable bunch of code. To accept the parameters, you must create a custom block, by performing the following steps:

1. Click on **Add Event**.
2. Go to **Advanced**.
3. Select **Custom Event**, as shown in the following screenshot:

You will see that a second event, simply called **Custom Event**, has been added to our list of events, as shown in the following screenshot:

Now, double-click on the **Custom Event** in the events stack to change its label to `Obj Click Check` (for readability purposes, this does not affect the event's name in the code and is completely ignored by Stencyl), as shown in the following screenshot:

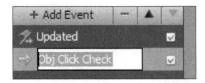

Now, let's set the name, as it will be used in the code. Click between **when** and **happens**, and insert the `ObjectClickCheck` name:

From now on, whenever we want to call this custom event in our code, we will refer to it as `ObjectClickCheck`. Go back to the **When Updating** event by selecting it from the events stack on the left-hand side of the screen. We are going to add a special block to this event, which calls the custom event we created just a moment ago. Perform the following steps to add a special block:

1. In the blocks palette, navigate to **Behavior** | **Triggers** | **For Actor**, then click and drag the highlighted block into the canvas, as shown in the following screenshot:

2. Drop the selected block inside the **always** block, and fill in the fields, as shown in the following screenshot (please note that I have deliberately excluded the space between the Player and Handler in the behavior name, so as to demonstrate the debugging workflow. This will be corrected in a later part of the chapter):

Now, `ObjectClickCheck` will be executed for every iteration of the game loop! It is usually good practice to split up your code like this, rather than having it all in one really long event. This would be confusing and terribly hard to sift through when behaviors become more complex!

There is a chance to assess what you have learnt from this chapter so far. We will create a second custom event; see if you can achieve this goal using only the skeleton guide, which is mentioned later. If you struggle, simply refer to the detailed steps we followed for the `ObjectClickCheck` event:

1. Navigate to **Add Event | Advanced | Custom Event**. A new event will appear at the bottom of the events pane.

2. Double-click on the event in the events pane to change its label to `Handle Dir Clicks` for readability purposes.

3. Between **when** and **happens**, enter the `HandleDirectionClicks` name. This is the handle we will use to refer to this event in the code.

4. Go back to the **Updated** event. Right-click on the **trigger event in behavior for self** block that is already in the **always** block, and select **Copy** from the menu.

5. Right-click anywhere on the canvas, and select **Paste** from the menu to create an exact duplicate of the block.

6. Change the event being triggered from `ObjectClickCheck` to `HandleDirectionClicks`. Keep the `PlayerHandler` value for the **behavior** field.

7. Drag and drop the new block so that it sits immediately under the original.

> Holding *Alt* on the keyboard, and clicking and dragging on a block, creates a duplicate of that block.

Were you successful? If so, you should see these changes and additions in your behavior (note that the order of the events in the events pane does not affect the game logic, or the order in which the code is executed), as shown in the following screenshot:

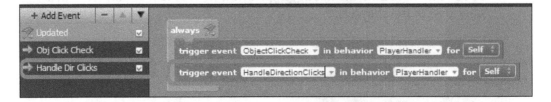

Learning to create and utilize custom events in Stencyl is a huge step toward mastering the tool, so congratulations on having come this far!

Testing and debugging

As with all the fields of programming and software development, it is important to periodically and iteratively test your code. This way, it's much easier to catch and repair mistakes. On this note, let's test the code we've written so far, using print blocks. Navigate to and select **Flow** | **Debug** | **print** from the blocks palette, as shown in the following screenshot:

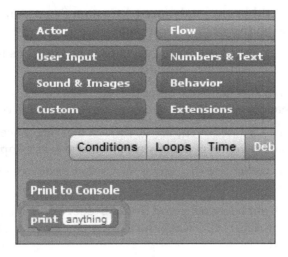

Now, drag a copy of this block into both of your custom events, snapping it neatly into the **when happens** block as you do so. Name them as follows:

- For the `ObjectClickCheck` event, type `Object Click Detected` in the print block

- For the `HandleDirectionClicks` event, type `Directional Click Detected` in the print block

We are almost ready to test our code. Since this is an Actor Behavior, however, and we have not yet attached it to our Cowboy actor, nothing would happen if we ran the code. We must also add an instance of the Cowboy actor to our scene by performing the following steps:

1. Click on the **Attach to Actor Type** button at the top-right section of the blocks palette, as shown in the following screenshot:

2. Choose the **Cowboy** actor from the ensuing list, and click on **OK** to commit.

3. Go back to the **Dashboard**, and open up the **Level 1 scene**.

4. In the **Palette** on the right-hand side of the screen, switch from **Tiles** to **Actors**, and select the **Cowboy** actor:

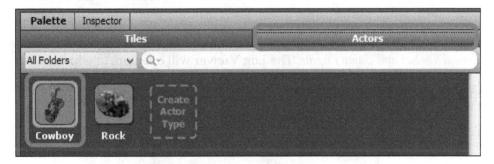

5. Ensure that **Layer 0** is selected (as actors cannot be placed on the background layers). Click on the canvas to place an instance of the actor in the scene, then click on the **Inspector** tab, and change the **X** and **Y Scale** of the actor to 0.8:

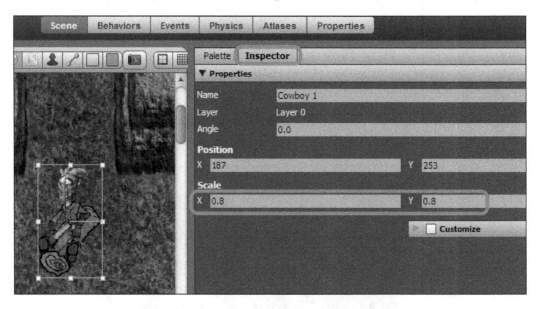

Well done! You've just added your first behavior to an actor type and added your first actor instance to a scene! We are now ready to test our code. First, click on the **Log Viewer** button on the toolbar, as shown in the following screenshot:

This will launch the **Log Viewer**, which we examined briefly in *Chapter 1, Exploring the Stencyl Toolset and Game Engine*. The **Log Viewer** will open up, at which point we need to only set **Platform** to **Flash (Player)**, and click on the **Test Game** button to compile and execute our code, as shown in the following screenshot:

After a few moments, if you have followed all of the steps correctly, you will see that the game window opens on the screen, and a number of events appear on the **Log Viewer**. However, none of these events have anything to do with the print blocks that we added to our custom events. Hence, something has gone wrong and must be debugged. What could it be? Well, since the blocks simply are not executing, it's likely a typo of some kind. Let's take a look at the Player Handler again, and you'll see that within the **Updated** event, we've referred to the **behavior** name as `PlayerHandler` in both the **trigger event** blocks with no space inserted between the words `Player` and `Handler`, as shown in the following screenshot:

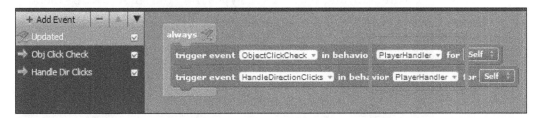

Update both of these fields to `Player Handler` and be sure to include the space this time so that it looks like the following screenshot (to avoid a recurrence of this error, you may wish to use the drop-down menu by clicking on the downward grey arrow, then selecting **Behavior Names** to choose your behavior from a comprehensive list):

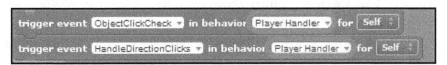

Great work! You've successfully completed your first bit of debugging in Stencyl. Click on the **Test Game** button again. After the game window opens, if you scroll down to the bottom of the **Log Viewer**, you should see the following events piling up:

These **INFO** events are being triggered by the print blocks that we inserted into our custom events, and prove that our code is now working. Excellent job! Much of the rest of the code for the **Player Handler** behavior will be covered in *Chapter 7, Complex Behaviors and Code*. Let's move on to a new actor; prepare to meet Dastardly Dan!

Adding the balloon

Let's add the balloon actor to our game, and insert it into **Level 1**:

1. Go to the **Dashboard**, and select **Actor Types** from the **RESOURCES** menu.

2. Select **Click here to create a new Actor Type**.

3. Name it `Balloon`, and click on **Create**.

4. Click on **This Actor Type contains no animations. Click here to add an animation**.

5. Change the text in the **Name** field to `Default`.

6. Uncheck **Looping?**

7. Select the **Click here to add a frame.** button. The **Import Frame from Image Strip** window appears.

8. Change the **Scale** to **4x**.

9. Click on **Choose Image...** then navigate to `Game Assets\Graphics\Actor Animations` and select `Balloon.png`.

10. Set the **Columns** and **Rows** values to `1`, and click on **Add** to commit this frame to the animation.

11. All the animations are created with a box collision shape by default. In actuality, the balloon actor requires no collisions at all, so let's remove it. Go to the **Collision** context, select the **Default** box as shown in the following screenshot, and press *Delete* on the keyboard:

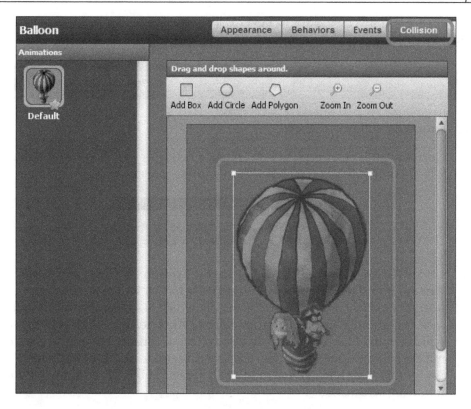

The **Balloon** actor type is now free of collision shapes, and hence will not interact physically with the other elements of our game levels. Next, switch to the **Physics** context as shown in the following screenshot:

Set the following attributes:

1. Set **What Kind of Actor Type?** to **Normal**.

2. Set **Can Rotate?** to **No**. This will disable all the rotational physical forces and interactions. However, we can still rotate the actor by setting its rotation directly in the code.

3. Set **Affected by Gravity?** to **No**. We will be handling the downward trajectory of this actor ourselves without using the gravity implemented by the physics engine.

Just before we add this new actor to **Level 1**, let's add a behavior or two. Switch to the **Behaviors** context as shown in the following screenshot:

Then, perform the following steps:

1. Currently, this actor type has no attached behaviors. Click on **Add Behavior**, which is at the bottom left-hand corner of the screen:

2. Under **FROM YOUR LIBRARY**, go to the **Motion** category, and select **Always Simulate**. The **Always Simulate** behavior will make this actor operational even if it is not on the screen, which is a desirable result in this case. It also prevents Stencyl from deleting the actor when it leaves the scene, which it would automatically do in an effort to conserve memory, if we did not explicitly dictate otherwise. Click on **Choose** to add it to the behaviors list for this actor type. you should see it appear in the list, as shown in the following screenshot:

3. Click on **Add Behavior** again.

4. Under **FROM YOUR LIBRARY**, go the **Motion** category once more, and this time select **Wave Motion** (you'll have to scroll down the list to see it). Click on **Choose** to add it to the behavior stack. You should see it sitting under the **Always Simulate** behavior, as shown in the following screenshot:

Configuring prefab behaviors

Prefab behaviors (also called as shipped behaviors) enable us to implement some common functionalities without reinventing the wheel, so to speak. The great thing about these prefab behaviors, which can be found in the behavior library, is that they can be used as templates and modified at will. Let's learn how to add and modify a couple of these prefab behaviors now.

Some prefab behaviors have exposed attributes that can be configured to suit the needs of the project. The **Wave Motion** behavior is one such example. You can select it from the stack, and configure the **Attributes** as follows:

1. Set **Direction** to **Horizontal** from the drop-down menu.

2. Set **Starting Speed** to 5.

3. Set **Amplitude** to 64.

4. Set **Wavelength** to 128.

Fantastic! Now let's add an instance of the **Balloon** actor to **Level 1**:

1. Click on the **Add to Scene** button at the top-right corner of your view. Select the **Level 1** scene.

2. Select the **Balloon** tab.

3. Click on the canvas, below the **Cowboy** actor, to place an instance of the **Balloon** in the scene, as shown in the following screenshot:

Modifying prefab behaviors

Before we test the game one last time, we must quickly add a prefab behavior to the **Cowboy** actor type, modifying it slightly to suit the needs of this game (for instance, we will need to create an offset value for the y-axis, so the PC is not always at the centre of the screen):

1. Go to the **Dashboard**, and double-click on the **Cowboy** actor type from the **Actor Types** list.

2. Switch to the **Behaviors** context.

3. Click on **Add Behavior**, as you did previously when adding prefab behaviors to the **Balloon** actor type.

4. This time, under **FROM YOUR LIBRARY**, go to the **Game** category, and select **Camera Follow**. As the name suggests, this is a simple behavior that makes the camera follow the actor it is attached to. Click on **Choose** to commit this behavior to the stack, and you should see the following screenshot:

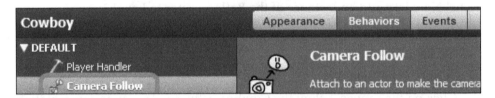

5. Click on the **Edit Behavior** button, and it will open up in the behavior designer, as shown in the following screenshot:

6. In the behavior designer, toward the bottom-right corner of the screen, click on the **Attributes** tab, as shown in the following screenshot:

7. Once you click on this tab, you will see a list of all the attributes in this behavior appear in the previous window. Click on the **Add Attribute** button, as shown in the following screenshot:

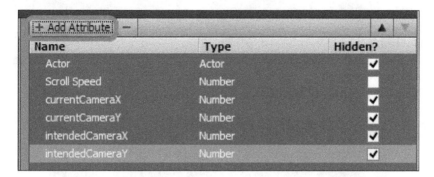

Perform the following steps:

1. Set the **Name** to Y Offset.
2. Change the **Type** to **Number**.
3. Leave the attribute unhidden.
4. Click on **OK** to commit a new attribute to the attribute stack:

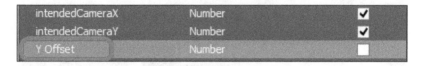

8. We must modify the **set IntendedCameraY to** block in both the **Created** and the **Updated** events, as shown in the following screenshot:

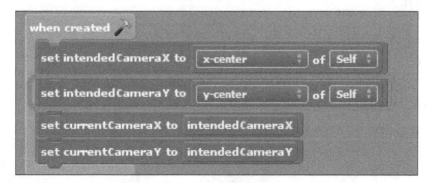

9. Hold *Shift*, click and drag the **set IntendedCameraY** block out onto the canvas by itself:

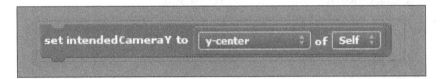

10. Drag the **y-center of Self** block out like the following screenshot:

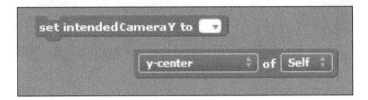

11. Click on the little downward grey arrow, on the right-hand side of the empty field, in the **set intendedCameraY to** block, and navigate to the **Math | Arithmetic |** Addition block, as shown in the following screenshot:

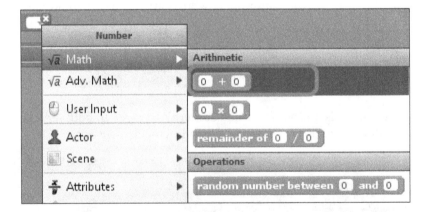

12. Drag the **y-center of Self** block into the left-hand side field of the Add block, as shown in the following screenshot:

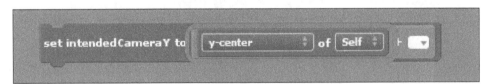

13. Next, click on the small downward grey arrow to the right of the right-hand side field of the addition block to bring up the same menu as before. This time, go to **Attributes**, and select **Y Offset**, as shown in the following screenshot:

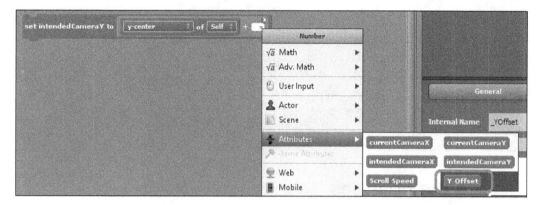

14. Now, right-click on the whole block, and select **Copy** as shown in the following screenshot (this will copy it to the clipboard), then simply drag it back into its original position, just underneath **set intendedCameraX to**:

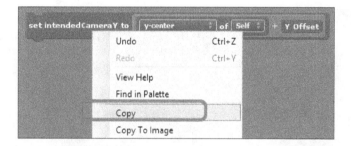

15. Switch to the **Updated** event from the events pane on the left-hand side of the screen, hold *Shift*, then click and drag **set intendedCameraY to** out of the **always** block and drop it in the trash can, as you won't need it anymore. Right-click and select **Paste** to place a copy of the new block configuration that you copied to the clipboard earlier:

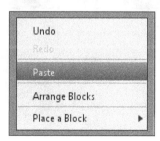

16. Click and drag the pasted block so that it appears just underneath the **set intendedCameraX to** block as shown in the following screenshot, and save your changes:

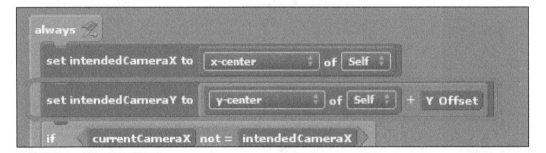

Testing the changes

Go back to the **Cowboy** actor type, and open the **Behavior** context. Navigate to **File | Reload Document** (*Ctrl+R* or *Cmd+R*) to update all the changes. You should see a new configurable attribute for the **Camera Follow** behavior, called **Y Offset**. Set its value to 70, as shown in the following screenshot:

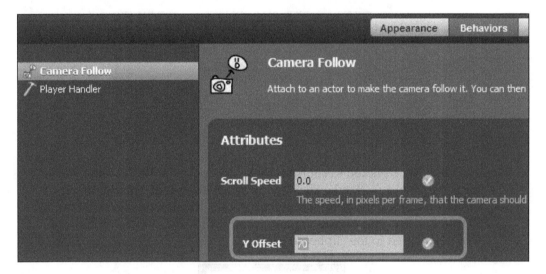

Excellent! Now go back to the **Dashboard** and perform the following steps:

1. Open up **Level 1** again.

2. Under **Physics**, set **Gravity (Vertical)** to 8.0.

3. Click on **Test Game**, and after a few moments, a new game window should appear. At this stage, what you should see is the Cowboy shooting down the hill with the camera following him, and the balloon floating around and above him.

Summary

In this chapter, we learned the basics of creating behaviors, adding and setting attributes of various types, adding and modifying prefab behaviors, and even some rudimentary testing and debugging. Give yourself a pat on the back; you've learned a lot so far!

In the next chapter, we'll continue to develop the code of our game to a higher level of sophistication, implementing the user input and game rules along the way. Let's keep this momentum going!

7
Complex Behaviors and Code

In this chapter, we'll build on the basic knowledge and competency that we acquired in *Chapter 6, Writing Simple Behaviors* with the Stencyl visual programming system. Going beyond the basic events and blocks, we'll learn how to:

- Create custom blocks and events
- Handle advanced conditional logic scenarios
- Communicate between the scene and actor behaviors using a series of special-purpose blocks built into Stencyl's proprietary visual programming language

Adding player interaction

Before there can be any ostensible gameplay, we must accept and react to some form of player input. This gives the player some level of agency within the game. Let's learn how to do this now.

Initializing the variables

The very first thing we need to do is initialize the values of our attributes. We can do this when the actor is first loaded into the scene, using the **When Creating** event. Let's add a **When Creating** event to the **Player Handler** behavior now by performing the following steps:

1. From the **Dashboard**, under **LOGIC**, select **Actor Behaviors** and open up the **Player Handler** behavior.

2. Navigate to **Add Event | Basics | When Creating** to add a **when created** event to the behavior, as shown in the following screenshot:

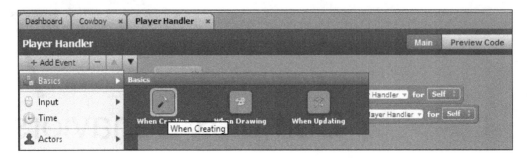

3. In the blocks **Palette**, select the **Attributes** tab, then click on **Setters**, and you will see a range of setters for each attribute, which we have already created, broken down into their attribute types, as shown in the following screenshot:

4. Scroll down to the **Number** attributes. Drag the **set Health to** block onto the **Canvas**, and then snap it into the **Created** block, as shown in the following screenshot:

5. Next, set the value of **Health** to **Max Health**, as shown in the following screenshot. This will initialize health to be equal to the value of **Max Health**, which we will set later.

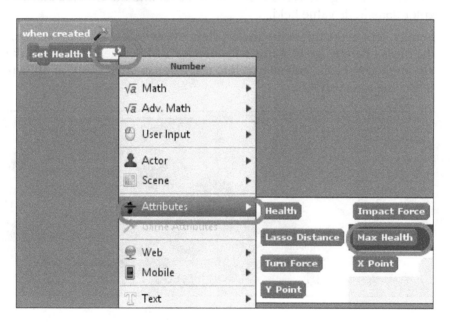

6. Now, under **Booleans**, drag the **set Can Be Hurt to** block into the **Created** block, and set it to **true**, as shown in the following screenshot:

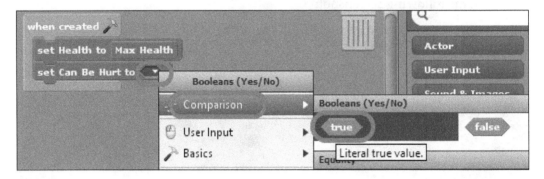

7. Do the same thing with the **set Draw Lasso to** block, but set it to **false** instead of true.

8. Do it again with the **set Mouse Over to** block, and set it to **false**.

9. Under **Text**, drag the **set MouseState to** block into the **Created** block, and enter None in its value field.

10. Finally, let's make this actor always simulate even if it is off the screen. In the blocks **Palette**, go to **Actor | Properties | Misc**, then drag the **make Self always active** block, and snap it into the **when created** block, as shown in the following screenshot:

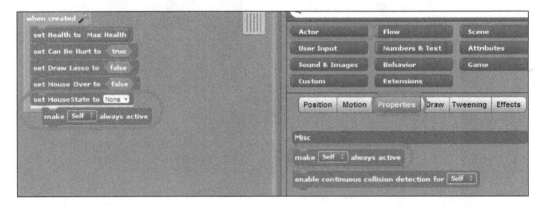

Handling player clicks

Great work! Now we're ready to begin writing the conditional code to handle the input. One of the key things that we need to establish with this part of our code is whether the player is clicking on an interactive object or not. If he is not, we treat the click as directional in nature. Let's start by writing some conditional logic and input code! Perform the following steps to do so:

1. Switch to the custom **Obj Click Check** event shown in the following screenshot, which we created in the previous chapter:

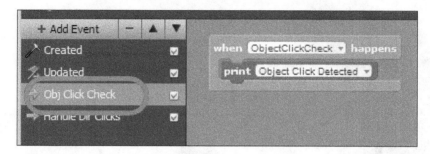

2. Navigate to **Flow | Conditions**, drag an **if** block out, and click on the **when ObjectClickCheck happens** block, as shown in the following screenshot:

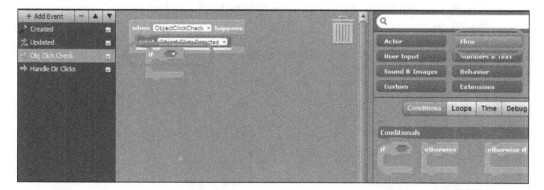

3. For the condition field of the **if** block we just added, we'll insert an **anything = anything** block to check for an equality condition. This block can be found by navigating to **Flow | Conditions | Equality**, as shown in the following screenshot:

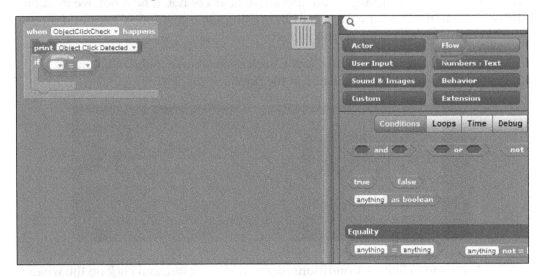

4. In the first field of the **anything = anything** block, let's insert a **Getters** block for the **MouseState** attribute (go to **Attributes | Getters** in the blocks palette to access it):

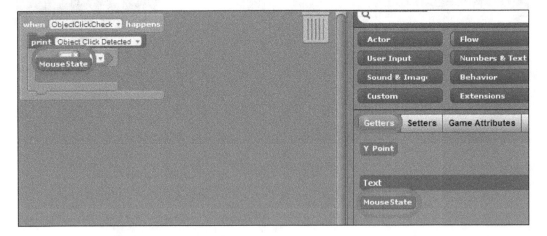

5. In the second field of the **anything = anything** block, enter the text value None, as shown in the following screenshot:

6. Great work! The next thing we will check for in our nested **if** statements is whether or not the left mouse button is being pressed by the player. Add another **if** block inside the existing one, as shown in the following screenshot:

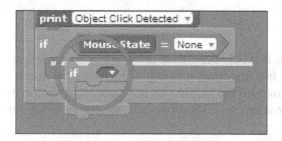

7. Now, navigate to **User Input | Keyboard & Mouse | Mouse / Touch**, find and add the **mouse is down** block, as shown in the following screenshot:

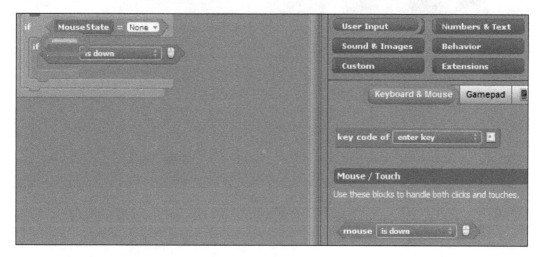

8. The next thing we need to do is insert a **for each actor on screen** block, which acts as a loop, to check a condition or a set of conditions for each actor showing on the screen for the current iteration of the game loop, as shown in the following screenshot:

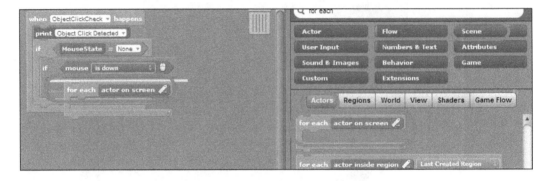

9. Add another **if** block. For this **if** statement's condition, we'll use another input block, but this time, instead of the **mouse is down** block, we'll use **mouse is down on** that allows us to check whether the mouse is over a certain actor when it is being pressed, as shown in the following screenshot:

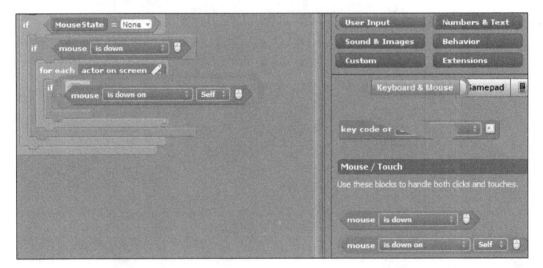

10. You will notice that the **for each actor on screen** block has an embedded **actor on screen** reference block, as seen in the previous screenshot. The next thing we need to do is drag a copy of this reference block into the **Self** field of the **mouse is down on** block, as shown in the following screenshot:

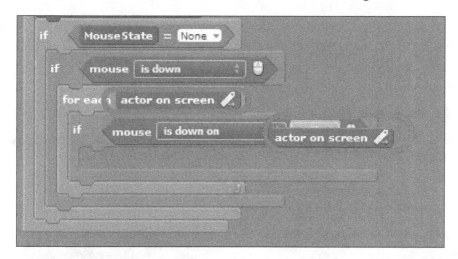

11. Now we'll use a **Setter** block for the **Mouse Over** attribute, which is a Boolean attribute, and hence can only be set to either true or false. Let's set it to **true**, as shown in the following screenshot:

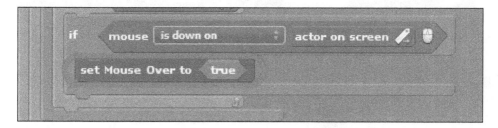

12. Now we must create a series of **if** statements, which check what type of an actor the player has clicked on, and react accordingly. Add another **if** statement beneath the **set Mouse Over to** block, which we added a moment ago.

13. Next, add an **anything = anything** block to the condition field for this **if** block, as shown in the following screenshot:

14. In the first field of the **anything = anything** block, let's insert a **type of** block, as shown in the following screenshot:

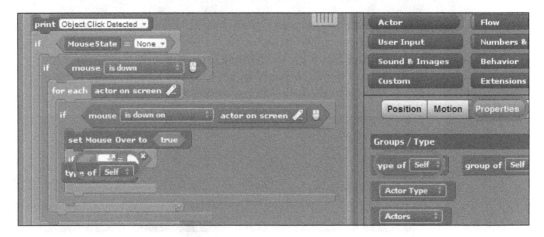

15. Next, drag another copy of the **actor on screen** reference block into the field called **Self** for the **type of** block, as shown in the following screenshot:

16. In the second field of the **anything = anything** block, we will insert an **Actor Type** block, as shown in the following screenshot:

17. Click on the **Actor Type** field within the block we just placed, and select **Choose Actor Type**.

18. A menu that contains all of the **Actor Types** within our game so far will be presented. Choose the **Rock** actor type, and click on **OK**, as shown in the following screenshot:

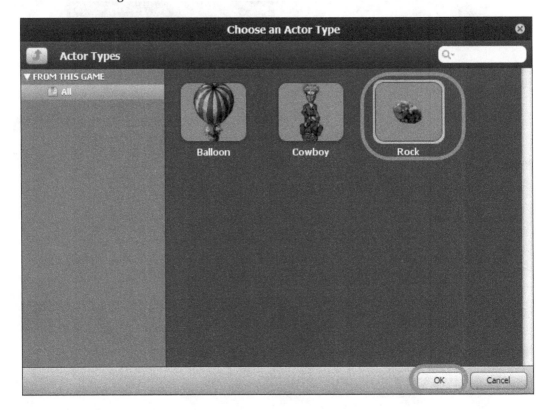

Our first custom block

Excellent work! You've just created some pretty elaborate conditional game logic code there! To make it work, though, we need to create our own custom block. Let's do this right now by performing the following steps:

1. Navigate to **Add Event | Advanced | Custom Block**, as shown in the following screenshot:

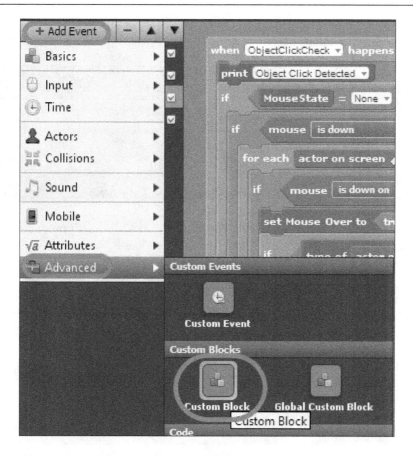

2. Make sure the new **Custom Block** is selected in the events stack, and click on **Create Custom Block...**, which will launch the **Create a New Custom Block** window, as shown in the following screenshot:

3. Set the **Name** to WhipAwayFromSelf.

4. Click on the **+** button to add a new block field, as shown in the following screenshot:

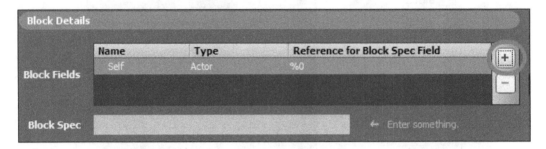

5. In the ensuing window, set the **Name** to OtherObject, **Type** to **Actor**, and click on **OK**, as shown in the following screenshot:

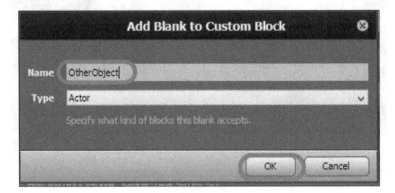

6. Set **Block Spec** to Whip %1 Away from Self. This %1 is a reference to the **OtherObject** field that we just added to our custom block, as shown in the following screenshot:

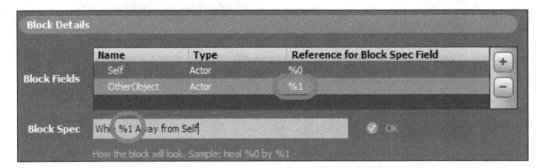

7. Leave the **Description** field blank and **Return Type** as **None**. Then, click on **Create**, and you will see the shell of your custom block appear. It doesn't actually do anything, other than accept an actor reference through **OtherObject**, as shown in the following screenshot:

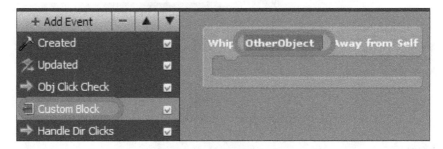

Now let's tell our new custom block what to do when **Whip OtherObject Away from Self** is called, by performing the following steps:

1. Go to **Attributes** in the blocks palette, and under **Setters**, drag the **set Target Actor to** block into **Whip OtherObject Away from Self**. Drag a copy of the **OtherObject** reference block into the **Self** field for the **Setter** that we just added, as shown in the following screenshot:

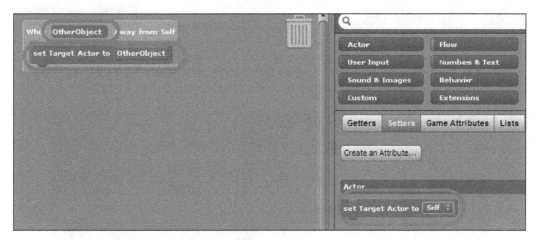

2. Now we must use a physics block. How exciting! In the **Palette** blocks, navigate to **Actor | Motion | Force**, find and add the **push** block highlighted in the following screenshot:

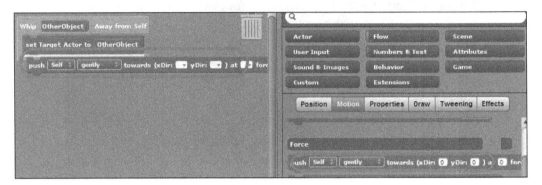

3. Drag a copy of the **OtherObject** reference block into the **Self** field of the **push** block.

4. Add a **subtract (-)** block to **xDir**, as shown in the following screenshot:

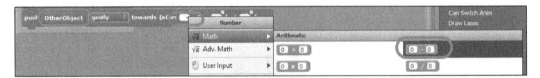

5. On the left-hand side field of the - block, add an **x of mouse** block, as shown in the following screenshot:

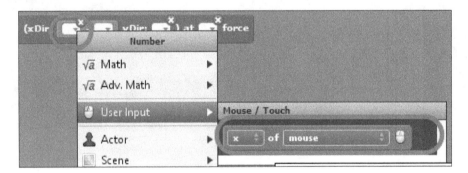

6. Next, on the right-hand-side field, add an **x of self** block, as shown in the following screenshot:

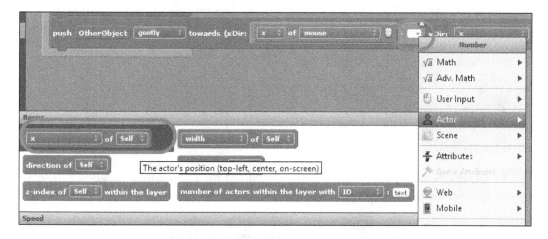

7. Click on the **x** drop-down menu in the **x of self** block, and change the value to **x (on screen)**, as shown in the following screenshot:

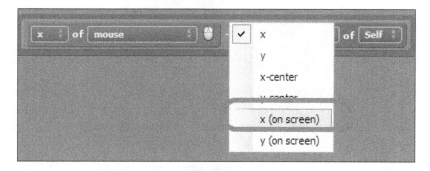

8. We'll be doing something similar with the **yDir** field of the **push** block. Follow the same steps we just used for the **xDir** field, but change the values to the corresponding **y of mouse** and **y (on screen)** drop-down options. What you create should match this exactly, as shown in the following screenshot (you could copy the contents of the xDir field by holding *Alt* and left-click, dragging to the **yDir field** to speed things up):

9. Now we need to provide a **force** value. Let's set the **force** to 400.

10. We'll add one extra physical force to the affected object before we move on to handle the directional clicks. We must manipulate the object's angular velocity. To do this, navigate to **Actor | Motion | Turning Speed**, and add a **set turning speed to** block underneath the existing **push** block, as shown in the following screenshot:

11. Add a multiplication block to the **to** field of the **set turning speed to** block, as shown in the following screenshot:

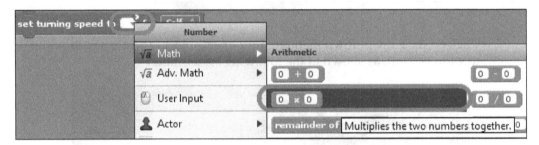

12. In the first field of the multiplication block, we'll insert the value 100. In the second field, we'll insert a **random number between** block (found by navigating to **Numbers & Text | Math | Random Numbers**), and give it a range of -1 to 1, as shown in the following screenshot:

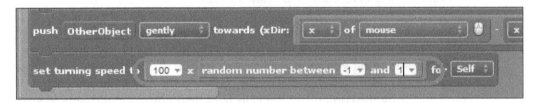

13. Currently, the **set turning speed to** block is configured to the **Self** effect, which refers to the actor this behavior is attached to. We must change this to **OtherObject**, which is a reference that we created earlier to the object on which the player has clicked. Drag a copy of the **OtherObject** block into the **Self** field of **set turning speed to**, as shown in the following screenshot:

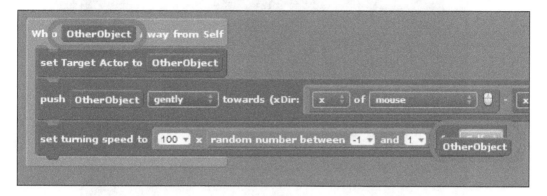

Excellent work! You just created your very first custom block. Now all that we need to do is call this block somewhere in our game loop, and we can whip rocks away from the avatar by clicking on them. This is our very first gameplay mechanic! To add the call to run the **Whip OtherObject Away from Self** block, follow these steps:

1. Switch back to **Obj Click Check** in the events stack.

2. In the blocks palette, navigate to **Custom | Player Handler**, and add the **Whip Away from Self** block, as shown in the following screenshot:

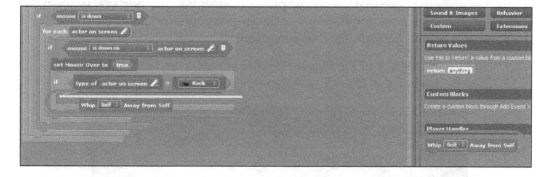

3. Drag an **actor on screen** reference block into the **Self** field of **Whip Away from Self**:

Great job! Now, when you test the game (go on, give it a go), you should see the rocks change direction and spin when you click on them. Just make sure you open up Level 1, and first add some rock actors to one of the layers. It feels good to see your game code working, doesn't it!

Handling directional clicks

It's time to write the code that allows the player to steer the **Cowboy** avatar down the mountain. This code goes in the second of the two custom events that we created in the previous chapter. Perform the following steps:

1. In the events stack of the **Player Handler** behavior, switch to **Handle Dir Clicks**, as shown in the following screenshot:

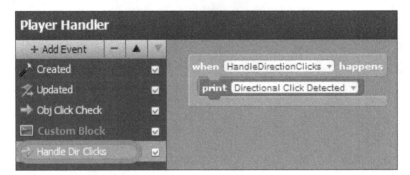

2. Remove the **print** block from **when HandleDirectionClicks happens**, as it is no longer needed.

3. Add the **if MouseState =** None and **if mouse is down** conditions, just as we did earlier for the **Obj Click Check** event, as shown in the following screenshot:

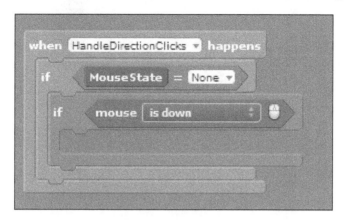

4. We must create a new custom event (navigate to **Add Event | Advanced | Custom Event**) that will calculate the direction in which the Player Character should move. Let's call it CalculateDirection, and label it **Calculate Dir** in the events stack, as shown in the following screenshot:

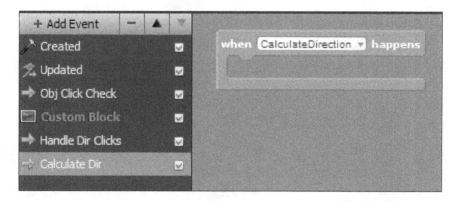

5. Add an **if** block and an **otherwise** block to **when CalculateDirection happens**.

6. Inside the **otherwise** block we just inserted, add another **if** block and two **otherwise if** blocks. What you have created should look exactly like the following screenshot:

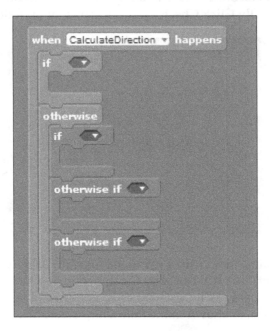

7. Add a < (less than) block to the first **if** block, as shown in the following screenshot:

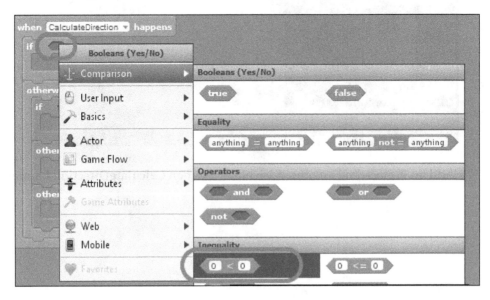

8. Let's put a **y of mouse** block on the left-hand side field of the **<** (less than) block, and a **+** (addition) block on the right-hand side field, as shown in the following screenshot:

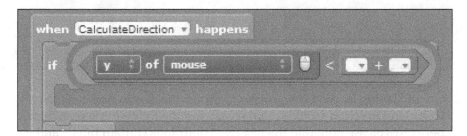

9. Now we'll put an **x of self** block in the first field of the addition (**+**) block, then change its drop-down from **x** to **y (on screen)**, and insert a **width of Self** block in the second field:

10. Change from **width** to **half-height of Self** using the drop-down for the left-hand value, as shown in the following screenshot:

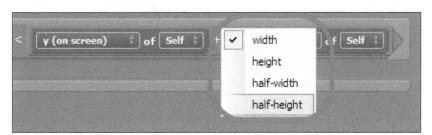

11. Insert a **set MouseState to** block, and give it the value `SlowDown`, as shown in the following screenshot:

12. Great! Having learned the process, your next task is to finish off the **CalculateDirection** block so that it matches the following screenshot perfectly (please note that the last two conditions contain plus 2 and minus 2 elements, respectively, to serve as a horizontal offset value):

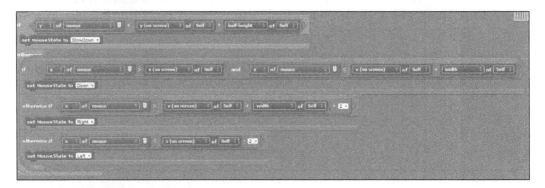

13. We're getting very close now! In the events pane, switch back to **Handle Dir Clicks**, and modify your conditional logic structure until it looks like the following screenshot:

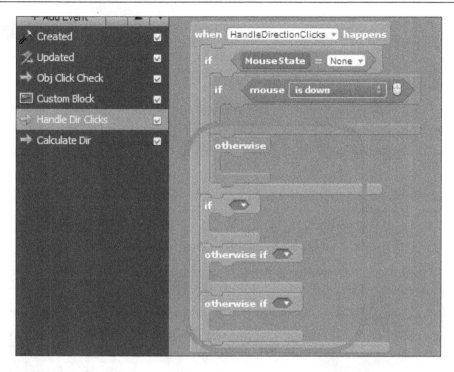

14. Navigate to **Behavior | Triggers | For Actor** in the blocks palette, drag out a trigger event in behavior for the **Self** block and place it inside **if mouse is down**. Set the event to CalculateDirection and behavior to Player Handler, as shown in the following screenshot:

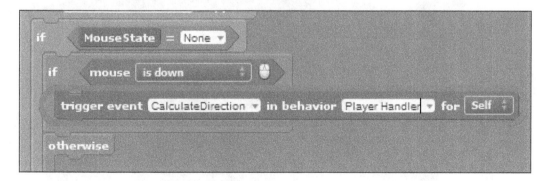

15. In the **otherwise** event, set the value of the **set MouseState to** block to None, as shown in the following screenshot:

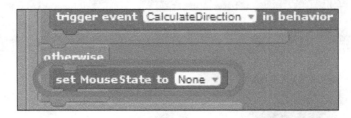

16. Copy (hold *Alt* and drag) the **MouseState = None** condition to all the four **if** and **otherwise if** statements. Do the same with the **trigger event** block. Change None for the **MouseState** condition to SlowDown, Down, Left, and Right, in that order, as shown in the following screenshot:

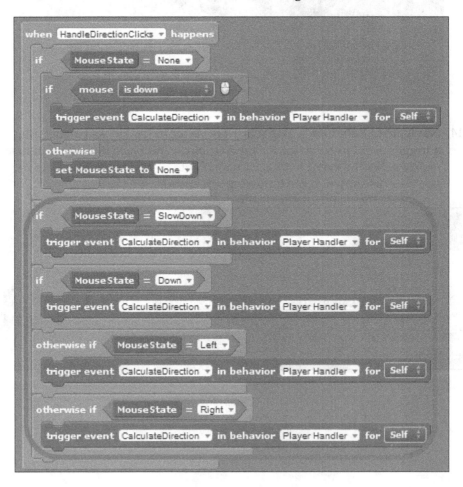

17. For the **SlowDown** condition, add another **if** block under the trigger event block, and give it a **>** (greater than) condition. For the left parameter, insert a **y-speed of Self** block, which can be found by navigating to **Actor | Motion | Speed**, in the blocks palette. Set the right parameter to 3, as shown in the following screenshot:

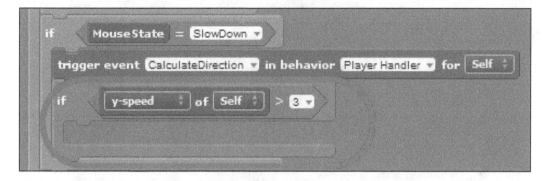

18. Insert a **set y-speed to** block (navigate to **Actor | Motion | Speed**), and then subtract 0.1 from the current **y-speed of Self**, as shown in the following screenshot:

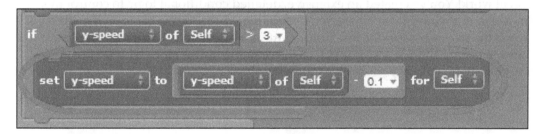

19. Insert four additional physics blocks and configure them exactly as shown in the following screenshot:

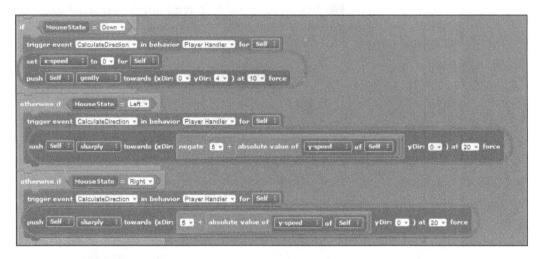

The when mouse is released event

Great work! You've created an extensive, detailed conditional logic to control the movement of your Player Character, depending where the cursor is on the screen when the player presses the left mouse button. You also created some complex custom events and blocks, enabling us to accomplish a lot more with far less code. Not too shabby! Now perform the following steps:

1. Now, we just need to create a **when the mouse is released** event to make our movement code functional, as shown in the following screenshot:

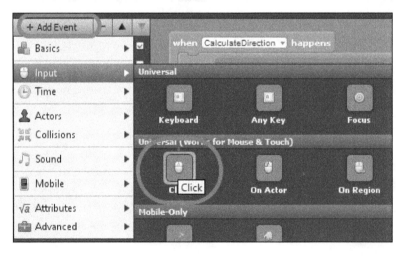

2. The new mouse event will be set to **pressed** by default. Let's change it to **released** now, as shown in the following screenshot:

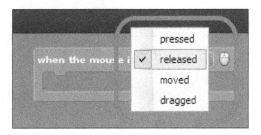

3. Add a **set MouseState** block to this event, and give it the value None, as shown in the following screenshot:

Now test it! If you followed the previous instructions correctly, you should see the Cowboy actor moving faster down the screen when you click below him, more slowly when you click above him, and sliding left and right respectively, when you click to the side of him. You've accomplished a lot so far, so be proud of yourself!

Switching animations

The last thing we need to do before we finish up in this chapter is switch animations as the **Player Character's** movements change, according to the code we just clicked together. In the **Handle Dir Click** event, perform the following steps:

1. Add a **switch animation to** block (navigate to **Actor | Draw | Animation**) to the **otherwise** block, as shown in the following screenshot, and give it the value Down:

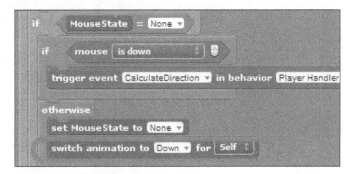

2. Next, insert the exact same switch animation block with the very same value in the **when the mouse is released** event, as shown in the following screenshot:

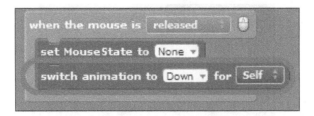

3. Finally, put one of these **switch animation to** blocks in every condition of the **CalculateDirection** event, and alter the values to Right and Left for the last two conditions, as shown in the following screenshot:

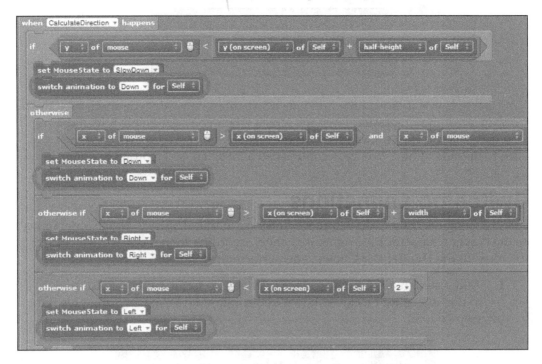

That's it! Test your game, and see the animations switching as you move the Cowboy around the level.

Summary

In this chapter, we took a massive leap in the development of our game logic programming skills by creating, from scratch, our very own game mechanics, utilizing physics intelligently, handling the input from the player in an intuitive and logical way, and we even created some advanced custom blocks and events. By now, I'm sure you're feeling much more comfortable and confident in your use of Stencyl, and I would suggest that, at this point, you consider starting a couple of your own experimental projects. However, don't quit just yet, there's still a lot to learn, so let's move on to *Chapter 8, Adding Sound FX and Music*!

8
Adding Sound FX and Music

We've come a long way by now in the development of the core game logic and mechanics of our prototype game. One thing that you would have noticed to be patently missing, however, is any and all forms of audio. Sound FX and music are important instruments in the hands of a game developer when it comes to sculpting an immersive and stimulating gaming experience. So what are we waiting for? Let's get auditory! In this chapter, we will learn:

- How Stencyl handles audio
- How to import sound files in MP3 and OGG formats
- The difference between sound effects and music in the Stencyl game engine
- How to play music in our game levels
- How to trigger sound effects on the fly

Supporting both MP3 and OGG formats

Stencyl supports two basic audio file formats: MP3 and OGG. One could be forgiven for making the assumption that this means we, as Stencyl developers, can choose which file format to use, according to our own preference. However, this assumption would be wrong. In actuality, the file formats are tied to specific target platforms. Here is the breakdown in a nutshell:

- MP3 is supported by:
  - Adobe Flash (Flash can also utilize OGG, but not through Stencyl, due to the limitations of the OpenFL framework, on which Stencyl is dependent)

- OGG is supported by:
  - Android
  - iOS
  - Windows
  - Linux
  - OS X

So in essence, MP3 is supported because the Flash targets won't accept any other format. The OGG format is used for everything else. This means two things:

1. If you're not planning to ever publish your game to Flash, you can stick with OGG and ignore the MP3 format. The only limitation in this scenario is that you won't be able to test the sound for your mobile games in the Flash Player, which is a useful thing to be able to do.

2. If you are planning to publish to Flash as well as other mobile and/or desktop targets, you will have to provide both the MP3 and OGG versions of your audio files. This may seem like a nuisance, but it actually doesn't take long to convert between the two formats, once you get used to it. This can be done easily, using applications such as Audacity (you can download this free online application from `http://audacity.sourceforge.net/`).

Importing audio files into Stencyl

Let's import our first few audio files into Stencyl. We'll import both the OGG and MP3 versions of the sound files so that we can publish them to Flash as well as the other target platforms. Perform the following steps to do so:

1. Go to **Dashboard**.

2. Under **RESOURCES**, select **Sounds**, and click on the **Create New** button, as shown in the following screenshot:

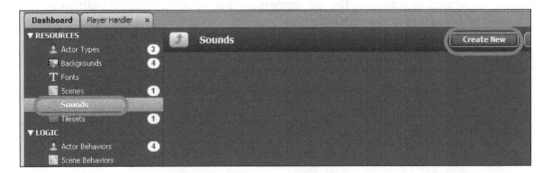

3.   The **Create New...** window will appear. Provide the name `Whip Away`, then
     click on **Create**, as shown in the following screenshot:

4.   The sound editor window will now appear. To begin with, let's click on
     Import MP3, as shown in the following screenshot:

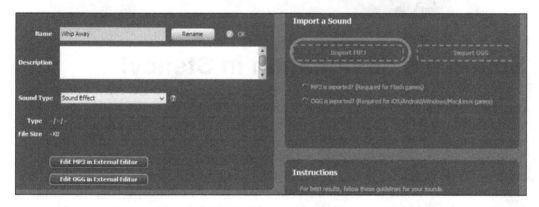

5.   A file explorer window will pop up. Navigate to `Game Assets\Sounds\MP3`,
     then select and import `whip.mp3`.

6.   Next, click on the **Import OGG** button, as shown in the following screenshot:

7. This time, navigate to `Game Assets\Sounds\OGG`, then select and import `whip.ogg`.

Excellent! If you see the two green tick marks appearing beneath the import button we just used, then you have successfully imported both the file formats, and they are almost ready to use this audio asset in the game:

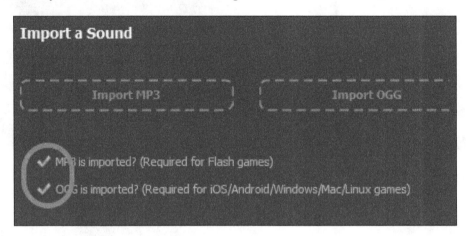

Sound file designation in Stencyl

Sounds in Stencyl must be designated as either **Music** or **Sound FX**. Why is this, you may ask? In general terms, this allows Stencyl to make certain assumptions about the size of the file, and how to treat it in memory. The audio engine logically assumes that the music files will be larger than the sound FX files, and so it loads them and keeps them in the memory for the duration of the game. Sound FX files, on the other hand, are assumed to be relatively small, and so are loaded into the memory on the fly when they are called from the code, and then removed from the memory again. All of this happens under the hood, so to speak, in an effort to improve the performance of your games, so be sure to use the correct designation for your sound files!

The whip sound we just imported is **Sound FX**, so let's designate it by setting the **Sound Type** parameter to **Sound Effect**, as shown in the following screenshot:

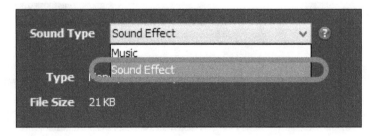

Great work! Before you trigger this sound FX in the code, let's import a music file by performing the following steps:

1. Go to the **Dashboard**, as before, and create a new sound asset. Name it Country Music, and then click on **Create**.

2. Click on **Import MP3**, then navigate to and import Game Assets\Sounds\ MP3\Country Music.mp3.

3. Click on **Import OGG**, then navigate to and import Game Assets\Sounds\ OGG\Country Music.ogg.

4. Change **Sound Type** to **Music**.

Playing sound FX and music in Stencyl

Well done! You have now successfully imported both music and sound FX files. Now all that remains is to trigger them in the code. Perform the following steps to do so:

1. Open up the **Player Handler** behavior, and in the events pane, switch to **Created**, as shown in the following screenshot:

2. In the blocks palette, go to **Sound & Images | Sound | Playback**, then drag out a **Play Sound** block, and add it to the stock of blocks in the **when created** event block, as shown in the following screenshot:

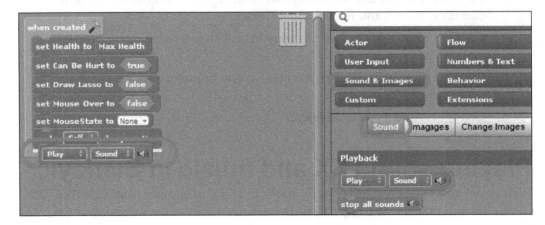

3. Change **Play** to **Loop**, as shown in the following screenshot:

4. Navigate to **Sound | Choose Sound**, as shown in the following screenshot, then select **Country Music**, and click on **OK** to commit, as shown in the following screenshot:

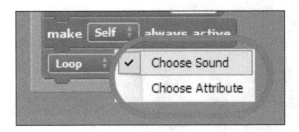

Now, when we test the game, **Country Music** will start looping at the beginning of every game level! Next, we need to trigger the **Whip Away Sound FX** whenever we whip a rock. Perform the following steps to do so:

1. In the events pane, go to **Custom Block** in the events list to the left, press *F2* and rename it to `Whip`, as seen in the following screenshot, to keep all of the event labels clear and distinct. Add a **Play Sound** block to the stack of blocks, which has already been added:

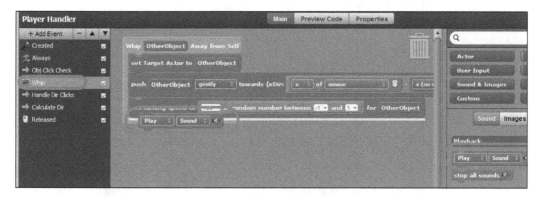

2. In this case, we'll leave **Play** unchanged, as it would not be desirable to have this sound FX loop.

3. Navigate to **Sound | Choose Sound**, and select **Whip Away**.

That's it, my friend! Test the game, and you should hear music looping in the background from the very start. What's more, when you click on the rocks, you'll hear the Whip Away sound FX!

Summary

In this chapter, we learned how Stencyl interprets and handles audio files, the reason why both the OGG and MP3 formats are supported, when you must provide either or both the formats, how to import sound files and designate them as either sound FX or music files, and most importantly, how to trigger these audio files in the game code. Well done on having learned so much in such little time! In the next chapter, we'll continue to polish our prototype by adding **HUD** elements to our game, and even animate these to add an aesthetic value to the end product. So let's get going; see you in the next chapter!

9
Adding HUD Elements

In this chapter, we'll add some polish to our game prototype by integrating some animated **Head-up Display (HUD)** elements, and we will make some modest improvements to the gameplay in the process. We will learn how to:

- Create a layer of **HUD** actors that sit statically on top of our game levels
- Animate the **Dynamic Cursor**
- Represent the game data dynamically through HUD elements
- Communicate between multiple actors within a scene using actor attributes
- Make an actor follow the position of the mouse cursor
- Switch between scene and screen space, using anchoring

The dynamic cursor

One of the most important HUD elements in our game prototype is the dynamic cursor. Put simply, this is a special-purpose actor that we will create to replace the regular mouse cursor. It changes the animation, depending on the current movement state of the Player Character, hence the designation **dynamic**. To create the dynamic cursor, perform the following steps:

1. Create a new Actor Type, and name it `Dynamic Cursor`.
2. Select the **Click here to add a frame** button to import your first frame. Navigate to and select `Game Assets\Graphics\GUI Elements\down.png`.
3. Change the **Name** of the animation to `Down`.

4. Switch to the collisions context. Select the default collision box, and hit on *Delete*, as we will not need to calculate the collisions for this actor, as shown in the following screenshot:

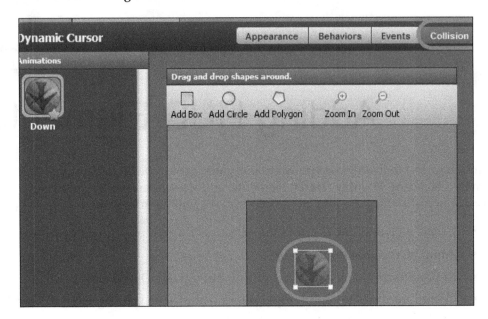

5. Duplicate the **Down** animation, as shown in the following screenshot:

6. Change the new animation's name from **Copy of Down** to Left.

7. Remove the redundant frame that is carried over from the **Down** animation, as shown in the following screenshot. You should have no frames in the **Left** animation after this:

8. Select the **Click here to add a frame** button to import your first frame. Navigate to and select Game Assets\Graphics\GUI Elements\left.png.

9. Duplicate the **Left** animation, and change the name from **Copy of Left** to Right.

10. Delete the redundant frame.

11. Select the **Click here to add a frame** button to import your first frame. Navigate to and select Game Assets\Graphics\GUI Elements\right.png.

12. Now let's add our fourth and final animation for the dynamic cursor. Let's repeat the same pattern as before and duplicate the **Right** animation.

13. Change the **Name** from **Copy of Right** to SlowDown.

14. Delete the redundant frame.

15. Select the **Click here to add a frame** button to import your first frame. Navigate to and select Game Assets\Graphics\GUI Elements\slow down.png.

16. Finally, we must disable all physics parameters for the actor. Switch to the **Physics** context, and configure the basic settings to match those shown in the following screenshot:

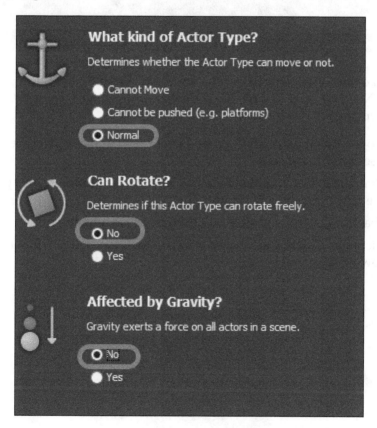

17. Now bring up the **Advanced** settings, and change the **Actor Mode** from **Normal** to **Simple**, as shown in the following screenshot:

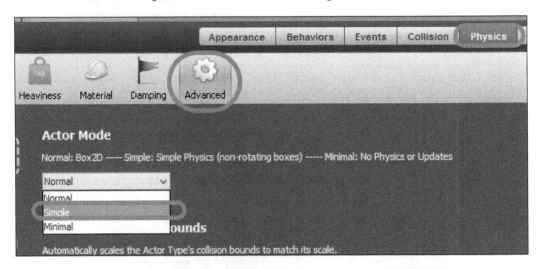

Brilliant! All of the animations have been imported, and the basic settings have been configured. Now, we need to write the code that controls our **Dynamic Cursor**. To do so, perform the following steps:

1. Go to the **Dashboard** tab, open up **Level 1**, and add a copy of the **Dynamic Cursor** actor to the scene.

2. Back in the **Player Handler** behavior, create a new attribute of type **Actor**, name it `Cursor`, and leave it unhidden.

3. Go back to **Level 1**, and click on **File/Reload Document**.

4. Click on the **Cowboy** actor, and bring up the **Inspector**, as shown in the following screenshot:

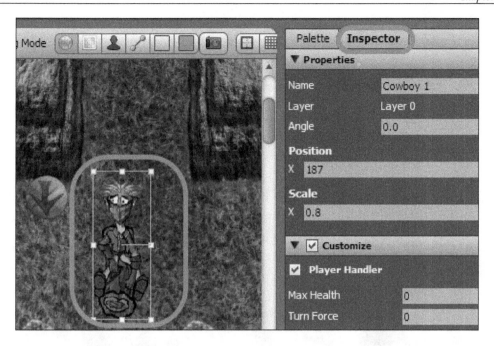

5. Tick **Customize**, and click on **Choose Actor...** for the **Cursor** attribute we added earlier, as shown in the following screenshot:

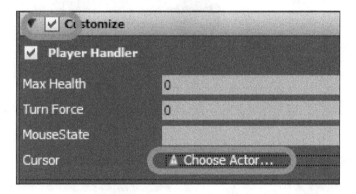

6. Select the **Dynamic Cursor** from the window that ensues, as shown in the following screenshot:

7. If all went well, you should see that the **Cursor** attribute now has the value **Dynamic Cursor**, as shown in the following screenshot:

What we've just done is assigned the **Dynamic Cursor** in the scene to the **Cursor attribute,** which we created in our **Player Handler**. This means that we can now interact with the **Dynamic Cursor** actor directly for that behavior, which is very useful indeed!

8. Let's switch back to the **Player Handler** again, and go to **Calculate Dir** in the events pane.

9. In the first **if** block, make a duplicate of the **switch animation to Down** for the **Self** block by holding *Alt*, then clicking and dragging it below, as shown in the following screenshot:

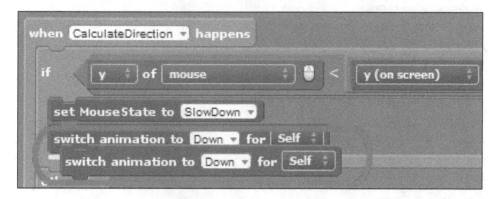

10. Navigate to **Self | Choose Attribute**, as shown in the following screenshot:

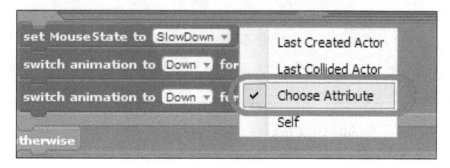

11. In the ensuing menu of the **Actor** attributes, select the **Cursor** attribute to which we assigned the **Dynamic Cursor** in **Level 1** earlier in the chapter. Click on **OK** to commit.

12. Now copy this switch animation block over to all the other **if** and **otherwise if** blocks, then change the animations for all the four of these blocks to **SlowDown**, **Down**, **Right**, and **Left**. As you do this, you may have to repeat the process of switching the target of this block from **Self** to **Cursor** for each copy, as we did earlier, as shown in the following screenshot:

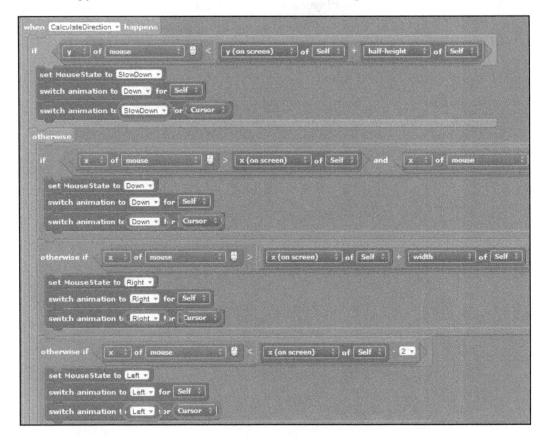

13. Switch to **Handle Dir Clicks** in the events pane.

14. Add a **switch animation to Down for Cursor** block to the otherwise block, as we did earlier, as shown in the following screenshot:

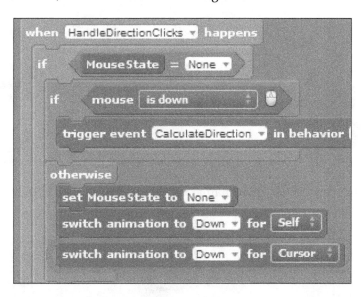

15. Next, we need to make the cursor follow the mouse position exactly. To do this, go to the **Dashboard** tab and create a new **Actor Behavior**. Name it `Cursor Handler`, and click on **Create**.

16. Navigate to **Add Event | Basics | When Updating** to insert an **always** event into the new behavior.

17. In the blocks palette, navigate to **Actor | Position**, and add a **set x to** block to our new **always** event, as shown in the following screenshot:

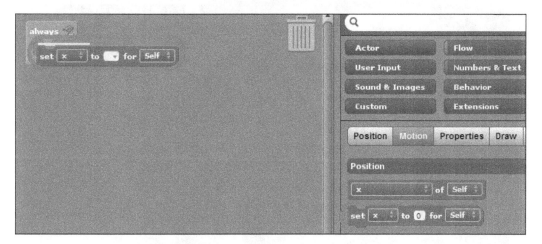

18. For the **to** field, click on the little downward grey arrow, and navigate to **User Input | Mouse & Touch | x of mouse**, as shown in the following screenshot:

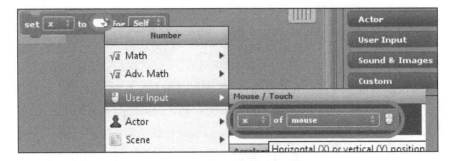

19. Duplicate this block, then change **x** to **y**, and **x of mouse** to **y of mouse**, as shown in the following screenshot:

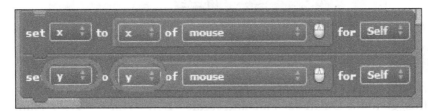

20. Navigate to **Add Event | Basics | When Creating**.

21. In the blocks palette, navigate to **Actor | Draw | Anchoring**, drag out and add an **anchor Self to screen** block, as shown in the following screenshot:

22. Next, switch to **Properties**, and add a **make Self always active** block, as shown in the following screenshot:

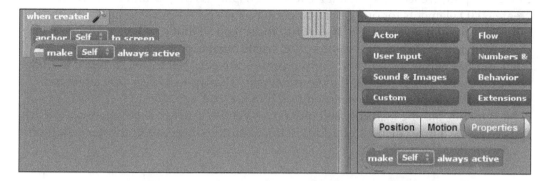

23. We also need to hide the mouse cursor. Navigate to **User Input | Keyboard & Mouse | Mouse / Touch**, and add a **Hide mouse cursor** block, as shown in the following screenshot:

24. Finally, click on **Attach to Actor Type**, select the **Dynamic Cursor**, and click on **Choose**.

Great work! Now when you test the game, you will see the **Dynamic Cursor** following the position of the mouse and adapting its appearance to the input of the player. In very little time, you've learned the basic process of adding an animated HUD element to a Stencyl game!

Summary

In this chapter, we learned what a Heads Up Display (HUD) is, and how we can create **HUD** elements for our games by configuring special-purpose actors to fit the bill. We learned how to anchor an actor to the screen so that it will be positioned on the screen, rather than on the scene space, create attributes that reference one actor from another within a scene and then communicate between them, and how to make an actor follow the position of the mouse cursor. That's a lot of learning squeezed into one little chapter! You've learned much so far, and you should be proud of your achievements, but the learning isn't quite over yet. Let's advance to where we'll learn how to create a main menu and add functional buttons. See you in the next chapter!

10
Adding Menus and Buttons

An intuitive and functional **Graphical User Interface (GUI)** is an essential element of any high quality, polished computer game. It is important that the visual style of all such GUI elements be intuitive and in aesthetic harmony with the overall style and theme of the game. In this chapter, we will learn:

- How to import and configure Actors that can be used as buttons in the menu screen
- How to program the basic functionality of such buttons
- How to create the overall look of the menu screen

Adding the scene and background

To create our menu screen, we will need to create a brand new scene, and then add a new background to this menu scene before we start adding our buttons. To do so perform the following steps:

1. Go to the **Dashboard** tab, select **Scenes**, then click on **Create New**, as shown in the following screenshot:

2. In the ensuing window, set **Name** to Main Menu, and leave all of the other values unchanged. Click on **Create**.

3. After a few moments, you will see a new, blank scene appear on the screen. Next, click on the **+** button in the **Layers** pane, and select **New Background Layer**, as shown in the following screenshot:

4. The **Choose a Background** window will appear. Select **Home Screen Background**, and then click on **OK**. You will see the background appear in the preview of your scene.

Adding the buttons

Now that we have created the shell of our **Main Menu** scene, it's time to start working on all those import buttons! Follow these steps:

1. Go to the **Dashboard** tab, select **Actor Types**, and click on **Create New**.

2. In the window that ensues, set **Name** to Play Game Button, and click on **Create**.

3. Click on **This Actor Type contains no animations. Click here to add an animation** button, and your first blank animation will appear for the button, called **Animation 0**.

4. Change the **Name** for this animation to Default.

5. Select **Click here to add a frame**, then navigate to and select Game Assets\ Graphics\GUI Elements\ play button.png.

6. Once you have imported this default animation, switch to the **Physics** context, and change the **Actor Type** to **Cannot Move**, as shown in the following screenshot:

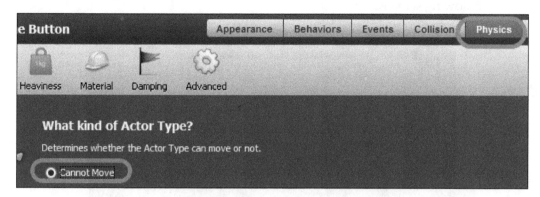

7. Now go to the **Advanced** settings, and change the **Actor Mode** to **Simple**, as shown in the following screenshot:

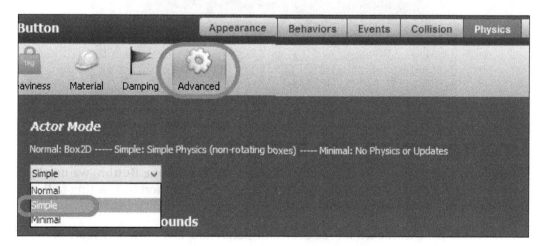

8. Finally, go to **Collision**, select the default collision box, and press *Delete* on your keyboard to remove it. This actor type will have no physical interactions of any kind, and hence does not require a collision box, as shown in the following screenshot:

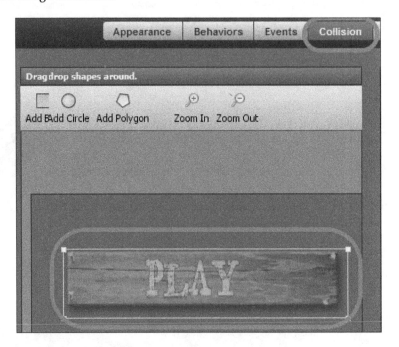

Programming the button

Great! Now that we have created and configured the **Play Game Button**, we must write an **Actor Behavior** that will cause it to behave like a button by reacting to the mouse's events. To do so, perform the following steps:

1. Go to the **Dashboard** tab, select **Actor Behaviors**, and click on **Create New**.

2. In the ensuing window, set **Name** to `Play Button Handler`, and click on **Create**.

3. Navigate to **Add Event | Input | On Actor**, as shown in the following screenshot:

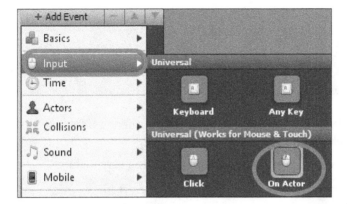

4. Switch the condition from **enters** to **is pressed on**, as shown in the following screenshot:

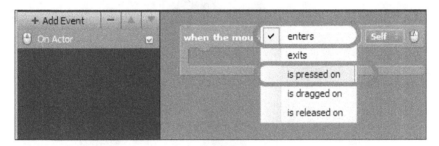

5. In the blocks palette, navigate to **Scene | Game Flow | Transitions**, drag out and add a **switch to Scene and Crossfade** block, as shown in the following screenshot:

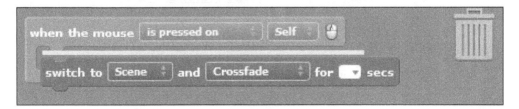

6. Click on the **Scene** field, and select **Choose Scene**, as shown in the following screenshot:

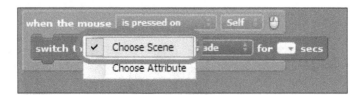

7. A window will appear, displaying all of the available scenes. Select **Level 1**, and click on **OK**.

8. Set **for secs** to 1, as shown in the following screenshot:

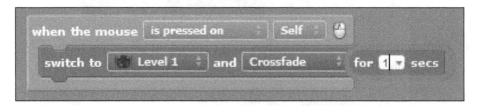

9. Click on **Attach to Actor Type**, and select **Play Game Button**, as shown in the following screenshot:

Great job! Now, we simply need to add the button to the scene, and test the game. To do so, perform the following steps:

1. Open up the **Main Menu** scene again.

2. In the **Palette** tab, under **Actors**, select the **Play Game Button**, as shown in the following screenshot:

3. Under **Layers**, select **Layer 0**, which is a tile and an actor layer, and then click on the **Bring Layer Forward** button, as shown in the following screenshot:

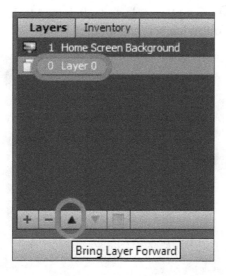

4. Make sure **Layer 0** is still selected, as actors can only be added to the tile layers, not the background layers.

5. Select the **Pencil** tool, and then click once to add the **Play Game Button** to the part of the scene, as shown in the following screenshot:

6. Now go back to the **Dashboard | RESOURCES | Scenes**, and select **Main Menu**.

7. With the **Main Menu** option selected, click on **Mark as Starting Scene**, as shown in the following screenshot:

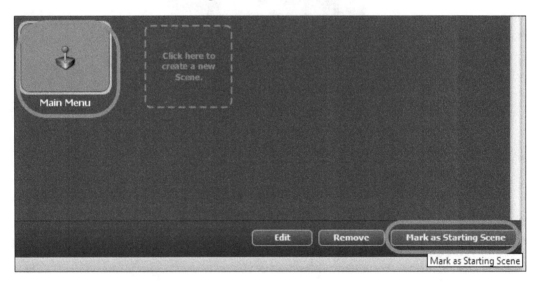

Now, when we click on **Test Game**, the **Main Menu** will be the first scene to appear. Go ahead, test the game, and try your very first button!

Summary

In this chapter we learned how to create a main menu screen, using the same basic game elements that, by now, we have become accustomed to using, including Backgrounds and Actors. We wrote a custom Actor Behavior to handle the basic functionality of the button, and switch to the first game level once the button is clicked. Well done on having learned so much in such a small space of time! Our educational journey still isn't complete, however, now it's time to move on to our final chapter, *Publishing Games and Monetization Methods*. See you there!

11
Scoring and Game Rules

In previous chapters, we incrementally learned about all the technical skills and knowledge necessary to build a game with Stencyl. We have even implemented some game mechanics. However, it would not be a game if there were no clearly defined game rules or gameplay. In this chapter, we will:

- Create and track a score value
- Render it to the screen
- Create a coin collection gameplay component to increment the score variable

Collecting coins

Before we can begin with programming the coin collection gameplay, we need an actor in our game that will represent the coins. Let's create one now, using the now familiar **Actor Type** creation workflow that we established in the earlier chapters, by performing the following steps:

1. In the **Dashboard** tab, under **RESOURCES**, select **Actor Types**, and click on **Create New**.
2. Set the **Name** to Coin, and click on **Create**.
3. Click on **This Actor Type contains no animations. Click here to add an animation**.
4. Change the **Name** of the animation from **Animation 0** to Default.
5. Ensure that **Looping?** is checked. It should be checked by default.
6. Click on the **Click here to add a frame** button.
7. Set **Scale** to **4x**, and **Resize Method** to **Bicubic** if these are not already set by default.
8. Set **Columns** to 6.

9. Click on **Choose Image...**, then navigate to and select `Game Assets/ Graphics/Actor Animations/gold coin anim.png`.

10. Click on **Add** to import this 6-frame sprite-sheet into our **Default** animation.

Coin collisions and physics settings

We now have all the visuals set up for our **Coin** actor. Next, we'll need to configure the physics settings. One thing we need to keep in mind is that, while we do want to be able to detect when the Player Character collides (overlaps) with a coin, we do not want him to react physically to this event (bounce, stop, slide, and so on). With this in mind, perform the following steps:

1. In the context menu at the top of the **Actor Type Editor**, click on the **Collisions** tab.

2. Stencyl has added a box collider by default. Leave it unaltered.

3. Under **Physics Properties**, check **Is a Sensor?** to prevent the Player Character from reacting physically when it collides with one of the Coin actors. Sensors behave like triggers; a collision is detected when the collision box overlaps with another, but the physics engine doesn't react to this detected event.

4. Switch to the **Physics** tab at the top of the context menu.

5. Under **General**, set **What Kind of Actor Type?** to **Cannot Move**.

Importing the font

Before we can render the score for our game to the HUD layer of our game, we need to import the appropriate font, otherwise Stencyl would use the default font, which would look pretty drab and boring. To import and configure the font, we need to follow these steps:

1. In the **Dashboard** tab, under **RESOURCES**, go to **Fonts**, and click on **Create New**.

2. Name your new font `Western Font`, and click on **Create**.

3. Under **Font Style**, click on **Choose**, as shown in the following screenshot:

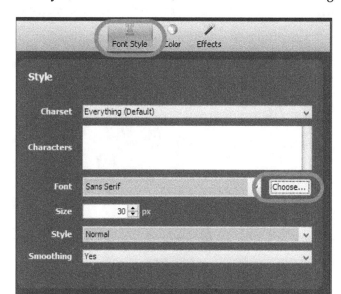

4. A file browser will appear. Navigate to and select `Game Assets/Fonts/GRINGONIGHTS.ttf`.

5. Set **Size** to `30`, as shown in the previous screenshot.

6. Click on the **Color** tab, then on the **Color** swatch, and set it to **Light Orange**, as shown in the following screenshot:

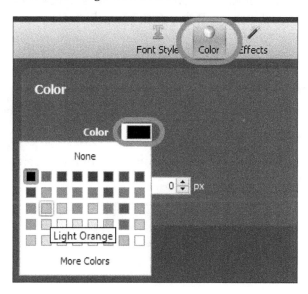

7. Next, switch to the **Effects** tab, and under the **Stroke** tab, change **Color** to black, then set **Size** to 1, as shown in the following screenshot:

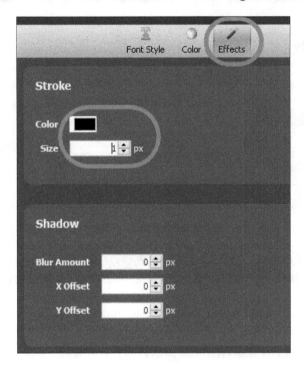

Excellent! Our font is imported and ready for use. The next thing we need to do is create the logic that will detect collisions between the Player Character and the coins, delete the Coin actor and increment the score, and ultimately render it to the screen using the font we just imported.

Coin collection

Let's start working on the coin collection code. To do so, perform the following steps:

1. In the **Dashboard**, under **Actor Behaviors**, open up the **Player Handler**.

2. Click on **Attributes** toward the bottom-right of the screen, as shown in the following screenshot:

3. Click on **Add Attribute** to create our new **Score** attribute, as shown in the following screenshot:

4. In the ensuing window, set the **Name** to Score.
5. Set **Type** to **Number**.
6. Check **Hidden?**.
7. Click on **OK** to create the attribute.

Now that we've created our **Score** attribute, we can start writing the code to detect the collisions with **Coins**, and increment this value accordingly. To accomplish this, perform the following steps:

1. Navigate to **Add Event | Collisions | Actor of Type**, as shown in the following screenshot:

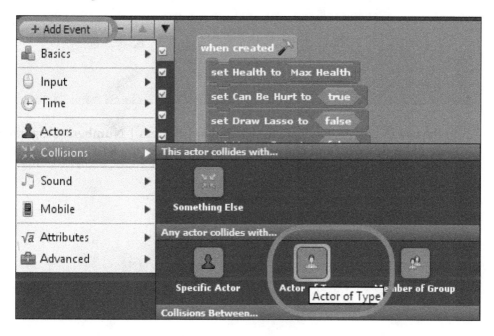

2. Click on the **Actor** drop-down menu, and select **Self**, as shown in the following screenshot:

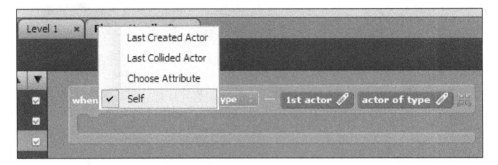

3. Click on the **Actor Type** drop-down menu, and select **Choose Actor Type**.

4. A list of all the available **Actor Types** will pop up. Select **Coin** and click on **OK**.

5. The first thing we need to do is kill the Coin actor. Add a **Kill** block (navigate to **Actor** | **Properties** | **Alive** | **Dead**).

6. Drag a copy of the **actor of type** reference block into the **Kill** block, as shown in the following screenshot:

7. In the blocks palette, navigate to **Attributes** | **Setters** | **Numbers**, drag out a copy of **set Score to**, and place it immediately below the **Kill** block, as shown in the following screenshot:

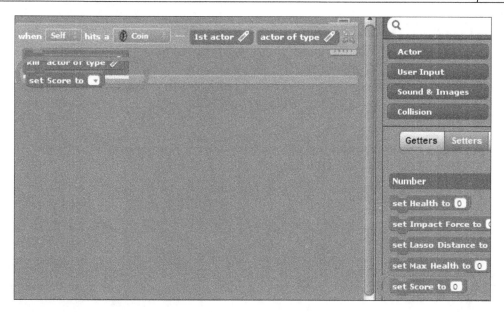

8. Add an addition (+) block to the **Score** block by navigating to **Numbers &
    Text | Math**.

9. In the first field of the addition (+) block, add the **Score** getter block
    by navigating to **Attributes | Getters** in the blocks palette.

10. Finally, set the second field of the addition (+) block to 100, as shown in the
    following screenshot:

Great work! Now, whenever the player guides the avatar over one of these **Coin**
actors, our code will **kill** the actor, and the **Score** attribute will be incremented by
an additional 100. What we have just built is the essence of a game rule. It is the
mechanism that will be used to determine the relative success or failure of the
player in the game.

Rendering text to the screen

Now that we have created the logic that tracks the score based on how many coins the player has collected, it is imperative that we render this information to the HUD so that the player can view their score as they progress through the game. To do this, we will use the font we imported earlier. Follow these steps to draw the score value in the HUD:

1. In the **Player Handler**, we must add a **When Drawing** event. Navigate to **Add Event | Basics | When Drawing**.

2. The drawing blocks are now visible under their own category, called **Drawing**, in the blocks palette. Drag out a **draw text at** block and snap it into the **when drawing** event block, as shown in the following screenshot:

3. For the **text** field in our **draw text at** block, click on the small, downward grey arrow to bring up the menu shown in the following screenshot. Navigate to and select **Text | Basics | Operations | Text & Text** (this is a concatenator, which means that it combines two strings of a text into one):

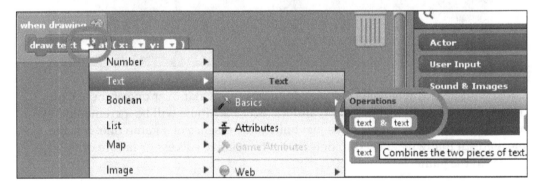

4. In the first field of the concatenation block we just added, please type Score: (don't forget to leave a blank space at the end). In the second field, insert a getter block for the **Score** attribute (by navigating to **Attributes | Getters | Number**), as shown in the following screenshot:

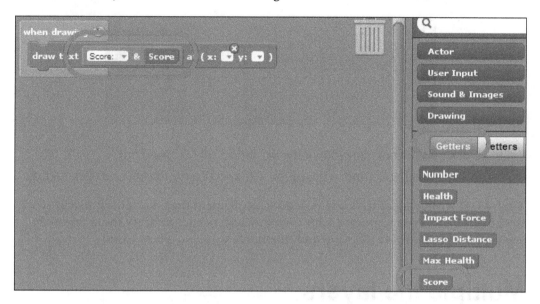

5. Set **x** to 5.

6. Set **y** to 5.

7. Now, we need to **switch to screen space** so that the text appears relative to the screen, as opposed to the actor. Go to **Drawing | Transforms | Space Conversion** in the blocks palette, then snap the **switch to screen space** block in at the top of the **when drawing** event, as shown in the following screenshot:

8. We'll also need to explicitly tell Stencyl to use the font we imported earlier. Snap in a **Set current font to** block between the two existing blocks (found by navigating to **Drawing | Styles | Color and Font**), as shown in the following screenshot:

9. Click on the **Font** drop-down menu, and select **Choose Font**.

10. A list of available fonts will appear. Choose **Western Font**, and click on **OK**.

You've just written all of the code needed to implement the coin collection and score tracking. You've even imported your own font and used it to draw the score on the screen in an aesthetically pleasing and functional way. Excellent work!

Multiple tile layers

All we need to do now is make a few small changes to our game level to get all of this working correctly. Follow these last few steps:

1. In the **Dashboard** tab, under **Scenes**, open up **Level 1** again.

2. You will see that we currently have two background layers and one tile layer. Actors can only be placed on the tile layers, which means, currently, all of our actors will be rendered to the same layer. This could create some ugly rendering anomalies regarding the z-order. To avoid this, let's add two additional tile layers by clicking on the following button twice:

z-order refers to the order in which sprites are drawn on the screen, so it is important to control which actors appear in front and which ones appear behind.

3. You will now see two additional tile layers at the top of the **Layers** stack (**Layer 3** and **Layer 4**)), as shown in the following screenshot:

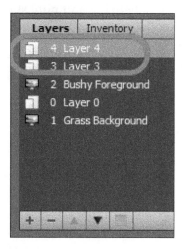

4. How we order our actors on these layers is going to be very simple. Place the **Air Balloon** on the very top layer (**Layer 4**) so it renders above everything else in the z-order (which is logical), by selecting it, then right-clicking on it, and clicking on **Bring to Front**.

5. Place the **Cowboy** on the next layer (**Layer 3**), by selecting the actor, right-clicking on it, and selecting **Bring Forward**, which moves it up in the order by one tile layer.

6. From now on, place and keep every other actor at the bottom of the tile layer, which is **Layer 0**.

7. Select **Layer 0**, then start placing coins (navigate to **Palette | Actors | Coin**) down through your level, so the player can guide the avatar around and collect them.

Excellent work! Now we are ready to test the game. When you do this, you should see that the z-order for the various actors is much better than it was before. Also, when the Player Character collides with the coins, the coins are killed (removed from the level) and the score value, which is drawn in the top-left of the screen, is incremented by 100.

Summary

In this chapter, we added a bit of polish to our game by importing and utilizing our own font to draw the score on the HUD for the benefit of the player. We also imported and configured a collectable object (the coin) and wrote the code to implement this game mechanic. In addition to all of this, we learned about working with text and drawing blocks, including space conversion. In the final chapter, we'll learn about what is involved in monetizing and publishing our Stencyl games. See you in *Chapter 12, Publishing and Monetization!*

12
Publishing and Monetization

Having learned the process of building a prototype of your game, you now have the necessary basic skills to go ahead and start working on your own game ideas, then flesh them out into full-fledged games—honing and building upon the foundational knowledge you have acquired by reading this book as you do so. If you ever want to become a professional, independent game developer, however, you will have to learn about and experiment with the game publishing and monetization options at your disposal. It is beyond the scope of this book to provide an exhaustive, step-by-step guide to set up a monetization system for your games, but we will explore the general process in sufficient detail so that you can get started with the process without the need to do a lot of additional research. In this chapter, we will learn:

- The basic process involved in publishing Stencyl games to the various supported platforms

- The key stores and marketplaces that are most established for the purpose of distributing said games

- The different monetization models, and how to implement them in Stencyl

- The necessary steps required to implement ads and purchases within Stencyl games

Mobile publishing and monetization

The **Proof of Concept** (**POC**) game prototype we developed in this book was conceptualized, from the ground up, to lend itself to both mobile and desktop targets. The gameplay and interface, however, are certainly more suited to the conventions of the casual mobile market, so we will focus on this publishing option. Mobile publishing also happens to be the most popular first choice for fledgling game developers, largely due to the low barriers to entry as well as the comparatively shorter development cycle required to create a quality mobile game, as opposed to a quality desktop game.

The two principle mobile platforms to which you may wish to publish your Stencyl creations are:

- **iOS**: Publishing to iOS requires that you have a developer's license with Apple, which, at time of writing, stands at **$99** per year. It is also necessary to purchase at least one modern Apple device for testing purposes but, preferably, you would have a modern version of both an iPhone and an iPad to test your games for both hardware specs and screen dimensions, using the most recent version of the operating system (iOS). If you intend to sell your game outright, then it would be a good idea to think seriously about publishing to iOS, as it is known to be a more affluent market, in which the consumers are more inclined to purchase games and apps outright.

- **Android**: The most popular Android app store at this time is Google Play, followed by Amazon, and Samsung Apps. I advice that you publish your game to all of these stores to maximize the exposure. There is currently no residual, or a yearly licensing fee for any of these stores, as is the case with the Apple App Store, although Google does charge a nominal, one-off fee of $25 to register as a developer for the Google Play Store. It is harder to make money by selling games on the Android app stores, as this market is known to be more spending-conscious as a whole when compared with iPhone and iPad users. Advertising and in-app purchases are generally the preferred monetization methods for Android games, although there are no hard and fast rules on this subject. The crux of the matter is, that if you want to sell your game outright, you'll have to do a really good job of convincing your prospective customers that the gaming experience will be worth the money.

Monetization with ads

Displaying ads within your games is one of the easiest monetization methods to implement. Be aware, however, that your ad revenues are not likely to be terribly high unless you achieve very large download and distribution volumes for your games. However, don't despair, as it can and has been done! Mobile game ads come in two basic forms:

- **Interstitial ads**: This type of an ad is usually large, or even full-screen, and appears between gameplay sessions—for instance, when transitioning from one scene to another. If the ads are varied and of interest to your key demographics, they are less likely to cause frustration for your players than banner ads.

- **Banner ads**: These ads tend to be relatively small, and offset either to the top or the bottom of the screen. They appear during gaming sessions. A word of caution here; if you overuse this kind of ad in your games, your players will likely become frustrated, and this can lead to low retention rates and even bad reviews, which will not help your game climb the charts. These are used sparingly, although they can be an effective means of boosting your overall ad revenue.

All of the blocks related to ads and purchases for the iOS and Android (mobile) targets are accessible and can be triggered in all **Actor** and **Scene Behaviors**. To do so, perform the following steps:

1. Simply navigate to **Game | Mobile** in the blocks palette, as shown in the following screenshot:

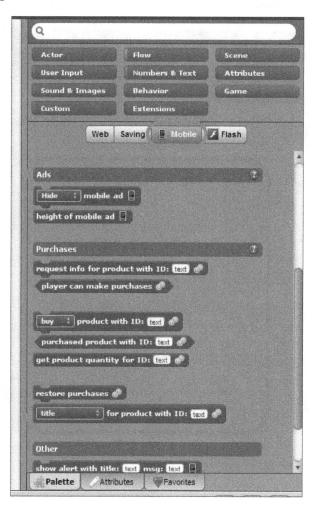

2. For these blocks to work; however, we must first provide some **API** (**Application Programming Interface**) information to Stencyl, in **Game Settings**. To find the **Monetization** settings area, click on the **Settings** button at the top of the screen to launch the **Game Settings** window, as shown in the following screenshot:

3. In the **Game Settings** window that appears, select **Mobile**, then **Monetization**. You will see two blank fields, **AdMob Publisher Key** and **Android Public Key**, as highlighted in the following screenshot:

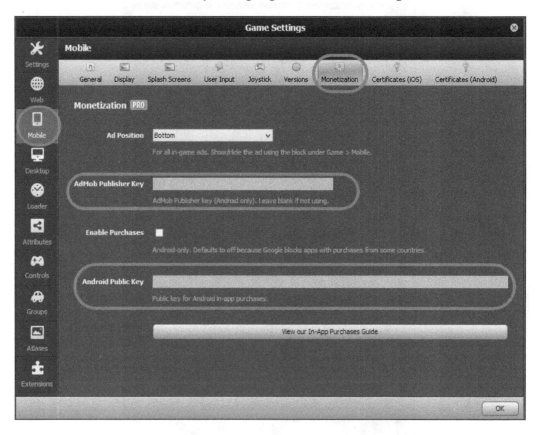

4. The **AdMob Publisher Key** is a unique **ID** that is provided to you when you sign up for an AdMob account—AdMob being Google's very own ad network for games and apps. You can simply copy and paste it from the AdMob publisher dashboard into this field to make the ad blocks functional.

5. The **Android Public Key** is an **ID** that is provided by the Google Play Store and is required to enable in-app purchases in your game. Simply copy and paste it over, once you have created your Google Play developer account.

For more detailed information about implementing purchases within your Stencyl game, click on the **View our In-App Purchases Guide** button, as shown in the previous screenshot.

Ad extensions

Stencyl supports the creation of third-party engine extensions that can be downloaded from the Stencyl website and integrated into your game projects. Many have already been created and shared freely by some hard-working, generous members of the Stencyl community, which add very useful functionality to your games, or enable the use of third-party APIs. Many of these extensions enable the use of various popular advertisement APIs that are not supported, out of the box, by Stencyl. Some of the most popular ones are:

*   **AdMob**: This adds an extended functionality (and iOS compatibility) to AdMob over Stencyl's built-in support

*   **RevMob**: This integrates RevMob ads into your Android games

*   **Vungle**: This integrates Vungle ads into your Android games

To implement a third-party extension for the purpose of enabling an additional ad network, for instance, follow these steps:

1. In the **Game Settings** window, select **Extensions**, and you will be presented with a list of all the extensions currently available in your installation of Stencyl. Hence, the list of extensions that you see will vary considerably from the one presented in the following screenshot:

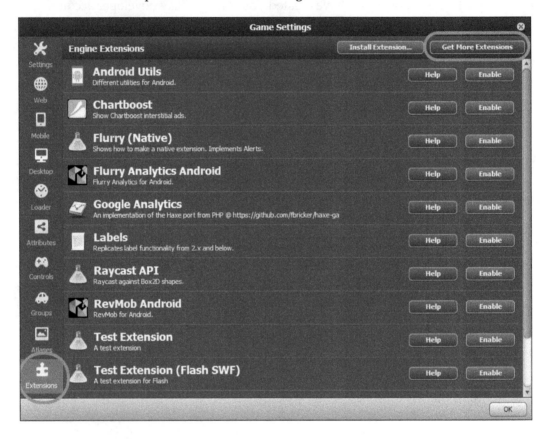

2. To find some useful ad extensions to install, click on **Get More Extensions**, as shown in the previous screenshot. This will take you to the appropriate section of the Stencyl website.

3. Click on **Download** for the **AdMob** extension, highlighted in the following screenshot. This extension improves the default AdMob support built into Stencyl, and even allows us to use AdMob with iOS so that we can utilize the same ad network on both the targets, as shown in the following screenshot:

4. In the forum thread that appears, scroll down until you see a link that says **Download AdMob Extension**. Click on it to start the download.

5. The downloaded file is called admob.zip. Back in Stencyl, click on **Install Extensions**, and navigate to and select admob.zip to install it. After a few moments, you will see it appear in the list of installed extensions. Click on the **Enable** button highlighted in the following screenshot, and then close and reopen the game for the extension to properly activate:

Open the **Player Handler** behavior again, and select **Extensions** from the blocks palette to see all of the new blocks that have been added by the AdMob extension as shown in the following screenshot:

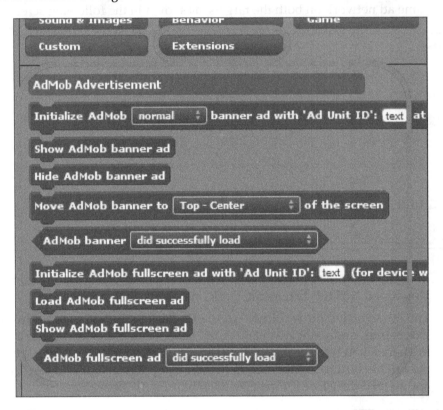

You will see from the preceding screenshot that this AdMob extension adds quite a bit of additional functionality to the default AdMob support provided by Stencyl. The two most significant additions are the ability to use fullscreen or interstitial ads, and the ability to use the same ad network and blocks on both Android and iOS.

Store certificates

Both Apple and Google require that you embed a certificate in your published game file, in order to be allowed to publish them to the App Store or Google Play, respectively. In the case of App Store certificates, the process is quite involved and beyond the scope of this 'essentials' guide. To learn the general process, I would recommend that you follow the guide provided by the Stencyl team at `www.stencyl.com/help/view/ios-getting-started`. In the case of Android certificates, however, the process is much more straightforward. Follow these steps:

1. In the **Game Settings**, go to **Mobile**, then select **Certificates (Android)**. You will see the following screen:

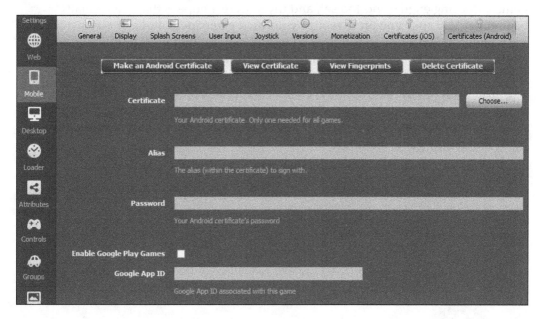

2. Even if you have never made an Android certificate before, click on **Make an Android Certificate**. You will have to provide an **Alias** (name), a **Password** (to keep it secure), your **First & Last Name**, **Company**, and your **2 Letter Country Code**. Once you click on **OK**, your certificate will be created.

3. Remember where this certificate is saved, and keep it safe by making multiple backup copies. You can use the exact same certificate for all of your Android games from now on, so you would never need to create a certificate again if you hold on to this one. Also, if you lose it, you may not be able to update your old games on Google Play, so keep it very secure.

Summary

In our final chapter, we examined the fundamental concepts behind game publishing and monetization within Stencyl. We also learned the basic process of setting up ads and purchases for our mobile targets, such as Android and iOS, in our Stencyl games. In addition to this, we also learned about certificates, why they're so important, and how to create one for our games. Hopefully, at this point, you're feeling much more prepared for going out and tackling some game development projects of your own, perhaps with a view to publish and monetize these projects in line with what we learned in this chapter.

It has been my great pleasure to help you come to grips with the wonderful Stencyl game authoring engine and toolset, and my sincerest hope is that these small beginnings will spur you on to realize your own game ideas and aspirations! If you are wondering where to go from here, I would suggest that you seriously consider joining the Stencyl online forums and get involved with the community there, as this is one of the best ways to learn the deeper aspects of Stencyl development. You may also want to visit www.cybermythstudios.com, where you can find even more of my online courses and books, which may aid you in further refining your game development knowledge and skills, if you so desire. Thank you for reading this book, and happy game making!

Index

Thank you for buying
Stencyl Essentials

About Packt Publishing

Packt, pronounced 'packed', published its first book, *Mastering phpMyAdmin for Effective MySQL Management*, in April 2004, and subsequently continued to specialize in publishing highly focused books on specific technologies and solutions.

Our books and publications share the experiences of your fellow IT professionals in adapting and customizing today's systems, applications, and frameworks. Our solution-based books give you the knowledge and power to customize the software and technologies you're using to get the job done. Packt books are more specific and less general than the IT books you have seen in the past. Our unique business model allows us to bring you more focused information, giving you more of what you need to know, and less of what you don't.

Packt is a modern yet unique publishing company that focuses on producing quality, cutting-edge books for communities of developers, administrators, and newbies alike. For more information, please visit our website at www.packtpub.com.

Writing for Packt

We welcome all inquiries from people who are interested in authoring. Book proposals should be sent to author@packtpub.com. If your book idea is still at an early stage and you would like to discuss it first before writing a formal book proposal, then please contact us; one of our commissioning editors will get in touch with you.

We're not just looking for published authors; if you have strong technical skills but no writing experience, our experienced editors can help you develop a writing career, or simply get some additional reward for your expertise.

CryENGINE 3 SDK
Level Design [Video]

ISBN: 978-1-84969-740-8   Duration: 02:14 hours

Unravel the complexities of the CryENGINE 3 SDK to create and design your own game level

1.   Get to know the various aspects of level design and apply them to create your first game level.

2.   Develop skills and game creation tactics that can be used with all types of games, and not just First Person Shooters.

3.   Learn tips and tricks not included in the online manual.

Learning Stencyl 3.x Game
Development Beginner's Guide

ISBN: 978-1-84969-596-1   Paperback: 336 pages

A fast-placed, hands-on guide for developing a feature-complete video game on almost any desktop computer, without writing a single line of computer code

1.   Learn important skills that will enable you to quickly create exciting video games, without the complexity of traditional programming languages.

2.   Find out how to maximize potential profits through licencing, paid-sponsorship and in-game advertising.

3.   Explore numerous step-by-step tutorials that will guide you through the essential features of Stencyl's powerful game-development toolkit.

Please check **www.PacktPub.com** for information on our titles

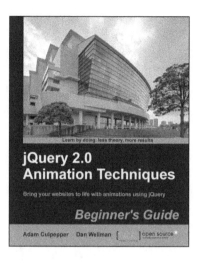

jQuery 2.0 Animation Techniques Beginner's Guide

ISBN: 978-1-78216-964-2   Paperback: 292 pages

Bring your websites to life with animations using jQuery

1. Get going with jQuery's animation methods and build a toolkit of ready-to-use animations using jQuery 2.0.

2. Over 50 detailed examples on different types of web page animations.

3. Create both simple and complex animations using clear, step-by-step instructions, accompanied with screenshots.

jQuery 2.0 Development Cookbook

ISBN: 978-1-78328-089-6   Paperback: 410 pages

Over 80 recipes providing modern solutions to web development problems with real-world examples

1. Create solutions for common problems using best practice techniques.

2. Harness the power of jQuery to create better websites and web applications.

3. Break away from boring websites and create truly intuitive websites and web apps, including mobile apps.

Please check **www.PacktPub.com** for information on our titles

www.ingramcontent.com/pod-product-compliance
Lightning Source LLC
Chambersburg PA
CBHW060600060326
40690CB00017B/3771